Advance Praise for Bountiful Women

An intelligent and exquisite book which compassionately and positively describes how the reader can become a bountiful woman. This is an inspirational read for anyone, but Dr. Bernell especially encourages large women to become "bountiful women" by learning self acceptance, resolving past and present relationship issues and opening to success in work, friendship and love.

Harville Hendrix, Ph.D., author of *Getting the Love You Want* and *Keeping the Love You Find*.

This bountiful babes' bible is a must-read for every woman who wants to be all she can be!

Pat Love, Ed.D., co-author of *Hot Monogamy*

Bountiful Women provides an incredible harvest for women who desire to accept and enjoy their bodies. The innumerable suggestions following the rich stories in this book are keys to a radiant life. This book is inspirational and yet practical—a wonderful resource for claiming energy, creativity, and joy, whatever your size.

Lana L. Holstein, M.D., Director, Women's Health, Canyon Ranch Health Resort, Author of *How to Have Magnificent Sex*

A life-changing book for anyone who's self worth is tied to a perfect body image. *Bountiful Women* is a must read for women who desire to break free of negative beliefs about their body and to experience positive and healthy self acceptance.

Joyce Nelson Patenaude, Ph.D., author of *Too Tired to Keep Running, Too Scared to Stop / Change Your Beliefs, Change Your Life*

Bountiful Women is a priceless gift, a must-read, for the large women of the world and the people who love them! It is upbeat and realistic, filled with practical information and creative strategies for physical and emotional wellbeing in a world that caters to the thin. Bonnie Bernell is an encouraging, warm, and wise companion who gives the kind of support every woman needs to take charge of her own life, to know that she is entitled to life's bounty, and to enjoy it to the fullest.

Bonnie is there with you every step of the way. She helps you to begin to live life now and to live it comfortably in your current body regardless of its size. She reassures you and answers the many "little" questions you never thought to ask. She gives examples of what others have done or said in similar situations. She shows how to meet the many physical challenges of a world designed for the small person, how to neutralize the inevitable self-criticism, what to do about the thoughtlessness or outright cruelty of others, and how to include travel, fun and romance as part of life.

This book is truly universal in its implications even though it was written for the bountiful women of the world. Many of us feel stuck somewhere. Most of us have something we want changed or some goal we feel we must reach before we think we are ready to live life fully. Many of us put our lives on hold. We're waiting until we've reached this goal whether it's a certain weight, a degree, money, a professional achievement, a level of psychological or spiritual maturity, or wisdom. This book encourages each of us to get on with life, not to wait for some idealized state of perfection or for just the right moment before we are entitled to begin to live.

Get this book and get on with your life; you'll be glad that you did!

Hal Stone, Ph.D. & **Sidra Stone, Ph.D.**, authors of *Partnering: A New Kind of Relationship* and *Embracing Our Selves*

We are told that perfecting our bodies will lead to the perfect life - well, these women have had the good sense to spend their time developing real skill at living. Bernell's gift is to make visible the everyday heroines all around us, the large women who prove through their courage, humor, and sheer *heart* that you do not have to be rich and thin to have a satisfying life. We are all, regardless of size, starving for these stories! I ate it up!

Debora Burgard, Ph.D., co-author of *Great Shape: The First Fitness Guide for Large Women* and founder of BodyPositive.com

Bonnie Bernell celebrates and empowers the lives of all women of bountiful proportions in this life affirming book. It includes 'secrets' that are gems and should be part of every person's emotional tool kit, bountiful women's courageous stories and life experiences, all mixed in with compassion, humor, and wisdom. The reader will find clear paths to satisfying our universal desire for acceptance and belonging.

Joanne Gaffney, R.N., M.S.W.

This book is dedicated to my pal and partner, Gary,
the sine qua non, *without which not, of this project.*

Bountiful Women

Large Women's Secrets for Living the Life They Desire

BONNIE BERNELL

Foreword by Carmen Renee Berry

WILDCAT CANYON PRESS
A Division of Circulus Publishing Group, Inc.
Berkeley, California

Bountiful Women: Large Women's Secrets for Living the Life They Desire
Copyright ©2000 by Bonnie Bernell

Publisher: Tamara Traeder
Editorial Director: Roy M. Carlisle
Managing Editor: Leyza Yardley
Copyeditor: Holly Taines White
Proofreader: Shirley Coe
Production Coordinator: Larissa Berry
Cover Design: Mary Beth Salmon
Cover Illustration: Nina Berkson/Link
Interior Design/Typesetting: Margaret Copeland/Terragraphics
Typographic Specifications: Text in Stone Informal 10/16.5,
    headings in Wiesbaden Swing Roman.

Printed in the United States of America

Library of Congress Cataloguing-in-Publication Data

Bernell, Bonnie, 1947-
    Bountiful Women: large women's secrets for living the life they desire / Bonnie Bernell.
    p.cm.
    ISBN 1-885171-47-1 (alk.paper)
    1.Body image. 2.Overweight women—Psychology. 3.Obesity in women—Psychological aspects. 4. Feminine beauty (Aesthetics) 5. Self-esteem in women. I. Title

    BF697.5B63 B47 2000
    158'.082—dc21

Distributed to the trade by Publishers Group West
10 9 8 7 6 5 4 3 2 1 00 01 02 03 04 05 06 07 08 09 10

Contents

Foreword

For over a decade I've worked as a massage therapist with hundreds of women. I've found that *it doesn't matter* what size a woman may be, we have all been taught to feel shame, if not disdain, for our bodies. Time and again, I've heard the question, "How can you stand to touch me, when my body is so . . . " Each woman fills in the ending with her private self-incrimination. Some believe they are too fat or too shapeless, no longer supple or attractive, or are perhaps scarred by surgeries or accidents. I've had clients who exercise frenetically, driven by a critical inner taskmaster while others sink into lethargy and "let themselves go." From time to time I've worked with a woman who has made hard-won peace with her body, but I've never met a woman who was thoroughly delighted with her body. Regardless of how closely our bodies align with the ideal we see in magazines, films, and on television, women feel lacking, unacceptable, even untouchable. It doesn't matter what size, shape, or age we might be—we all must grapple with this horrible curse.

This is not to say that some women don't suffer more than others. Those who land closer to the ideal may experience less overt discrimination. Most certainly, larger women are targets of regular criticism. Rather than ask the question, "Why don't you lose weight?" we need to ask questions like—"If over the half the female population wears size 14 or larger, why is the most stylish clothing designed for size 12 or smaller?" or "Why are armed chairs in restaurants and theaters designed for small rumps?" And "Why aren't car and airline seat belts designed to accommodate wider waistlines?"

The key word here is *design*. Larger women do not struggle simply because they are larger, but because, as a culture, we have designed our vehicles of transportation, our places of entertainment, and our work environments for the thinner half of society. Many of the problems bountiful women face each day could be alleviated by designing to include, rather than exclude, larger people. We don't design for bountiful people, we discriminate against them.

In response to this cruel judgment, *Bountiful Women* speaks out with a loving, accepting voice, conveying messages that are affirming and inspiring. *Love your body, whatever size*, Bonnie urges. *Stand up for yourself, even if you're different from others around you. Be who you are and stop trying to fit external molds* and *live in the moment and take risks, go on adventures—* these are affirmations of bountiful living, regardless of one's size. There's not a woman alive who can't benefit from Bonnie's wisdom, encouragement, and creative approach to personal challenges.

The most exciting aspect of this book is that it exists—resonating with truth in a world that reflects back to women a distorted ideal. Are you wider than you'd like? Too round in the middle? Have ankles you wish were narrower? Or thighs you try to hide? . . . all these so-called physical failings don't matter. Listen carefully as Bonnie tells us that we are loveable and acceptable no matter what. Be bountiful by accepting that you are beautiful just as you are. Any criticism to the contrary just doesn't matter.

—Carmen Renee Berry

Preface

I had to write this book. I have been thinking about or encountering the considerations in this book my entire life. I've been every size—from petite (last observed when I was a baby), all the way to bountiful, and every size in between. I was raised by a mother who modeled and always looked perfect. I never saw her with a wrinkled blouse, a run in her stockings, or her nails unmanicured, even when she died. My father was a physician who had definite ideas about how I ought to look and be. My body never matched their desires for me. I was told by family, friends, and an array of professional people what would make me and my body look good and feel better. No matter what I said or did, everyone else was watching and deciding what was best for me and my body. And I thought they were right.

As a young child, my mother called me BonBon, a nickname for Bonnie. I loved the name at first. However, as I entered my dating years, I discovered that bonbons were chocolate covered ice cream treats to be avoided at all costs. My nickname, like so much of my experience about my body, changed into something disappointing. As a teenager, I was convinced that I had to "weight" until I was thinner to be lovable. Since I was sure no boy would be interested in me unless I lost weight, I developed other talents such as my intellect, creativity, and being a good listener. I settled for being everyone's pal, seeing romance as something I had to wait to enjoy until I was thin, or at least thinner. When, to my surprise, people were attracted to me, I had trouble believing their intentions. All I had learned from so many people, including those closest to me, was that I had to be what they defined as attractive to be okay.

Through most of my adult years, my weight fluctuated dramatically. I did my best to become thin/thinner/lighter, whatever the euphemism for losing weight was at the time. I tried every diet plan available, some seemingly medically sound, some trendy, some unbelievable, but none of them effective for me in being thinner and healthier over the long run. I felt different from and less than thin people, having failed at these many diets. I was convinced that I was not entitled to living the fullest life possible.

While my parents and others might have inadvertently undermined my self-esteem, these experiences simultaneously served as excellent models for resiliency, speaking one's beliefs, and finding one's own way. Having found the traditional "rule book for a happy life" unhelpful to me, I set out with determination and energy to find how I could live life fully.

Today, I simply think of myself as bountiful—full of life, colorful, energetic, curious, sensual, sexual, and privy to all the opportunities the universe provides. I do what I need to do to feel and live bountifully, fully, and with gratitude for each day. I enjoy a rich, loving marriage to a man who is my friend and my lover. If I want to do something, I do it—and never let my current weight (whatever that may be at the time) get in my way.

I have been asked how I made the transition from self-limiting to self-appreciating. Some of my learning has been deeply personal—as a result of penetrating anguish that I thought would never end, and might even kill me. Other insights were accompanied by laughter that brought me to either hiccups or tears, both signs that the experience had completely consumed me. While I have found my own way, I have not traveled alone. I have learned from everyone I have met—important teachers—whether our contact was for a brief moment or endured a lifetime. Some of these teachers have been friends, others have been clients I've met through my clinical work as a psychologist. For more than twenty-five years, I have been awed and inspired by the resilience, sheer grit and determination, and stunning invention that my clients bring to their lives. The women, men, and couples with whom I interact each day have taught me that we all are capable of seeing ourselves as more. In addition, I've learned from the many bountiful women who shared their stories specifically to help me write this book—I have been truly inspired by these amazing women. My life will never be the same.

A recent *New York Times* poll said that about half the people in this country describe themselves as overweight. More than half are overweight according to the Center for Disease

Control in Atlanta. While reportedly 50 percent of the women in this country wear size 14 and above, we do not see large women in nearly that proportion. Where are they? Are they hiding? Yes. Are they "weighting" until they reach some imaginary right size? Yes. Are there ways they can handle those situations that have kept them from having a full life? Yes.

I do not suggest that life is necessarily easy, but nevertheless it is full of choices. We are not trapped by society's definition of us. Within these pages you may find a new idea, a new possibility, a new approach, so that almost any difficulty can be addressed from a different, more bountiful perspective. My hope is that each bountiful woman will see the myriad of choices inherent in every challenging situation. If you encounter what you experience as a wall, back up a step or two; you may see there is a totally different way to go forward.

Whether you lose weight, gain weight, or stay the same is not the point. The point is, live your life fully, richly, in whatever ways you desire. Rilke said, "You must give birth to your images. They are the future waiting to be born . . . fear not the strangeness you feel. The future must enter into you long before it happens. . . . Just wait for the birth . . . for the hour of new clarity." I invite you to become a bountiful woman, like the many women who shared their stories with me. The stories in these pages are true, although some have been altered to protect privacy. Join me, join us, and become a bountiful woman—who lives her life and stops "weighting."

By the way, a few of my close friends have taken to calling me BonBon again. Once more, as when I was a young girl, at peace with my body and unaffected by criticism, I am able to feel that delicious warmth of love and affection when my name is used. I wish the same bountiful life for you.

—Palo Alto, California

Section One

Me, Myself, and I

Become a Bountiful Woman

*To me, bountiful is a way of life—full, rich,
robust. While "overweight," "obese," and "fat,"
women may wait for life to begin or hide until
something imagined is different, bountiful
women move forward . . .*

Ever get tired of hearing people talk about weight? Catherine told me it seemed like "everyone talks about weight all the time, mine, theirs, Oprah's, the little girl's next door!" At the age of forty, Catherine, a retailer, has been many different weights over the years, and is acutely aware of other people's attitudes about personal size. She has heard friends and customers talk about their latest food plan, whether they were gaining weight or losing weight, even how much fat a restaurant meal contained. These people were deciding whether they had worked out enough to have dessert!

"The obsession with food—not eating, eating, what to eat, when to eat, fat, thin, large, small—it was all driving me crazy! And I was caught up in it too. I have done it all, every plan, every pill, every therapy, everything I've thought of, heard about, read about. I finally came to the place where it was time to be and enjoy who I am, including my strong, resilient, healthy body. I'll admit that I would like to be thinner, but I am not going to pay the price required to be thin. When I'm watching my weight, it seems like I can't see or do anything else in life. I can't be myself and be thin. So, I made the decision to accept myself at whatever size I happen to be." Catherine told me that she believed self-acceptance was the first step, the most difficult step, to confront in redefining herself.

As a large woman myself, for years I struggled with accepting and appreciating myself. Today, I do not define myself by my size, but by all that makes me who I am. I embrace my various parts, as a healthy person, an interesting person, a worthwhile person, a loving person, a lovable person, an entitled person, even a pain the neck at times. As a woman, or wife, or friend, or psychologist, or artist, I know I can be successful in each aspect of my life. My options are no longer arbitrarily limited because I feel undeserving or somehow a problem for someone else. I'm not alone in this experience. Many of us have allowed ourselves to be defined by others' negative views of size.

So how shall we define ourselves? Should we be identified as fat women, large women, fluffy women, obese women, women who are out of control, women with extra weight? Try some of these definitions on for size.

Some people avoid using the word "fat," which Deb, a forty-two-year-old psychologist, uses openly and easily. She said, "The word 'fat' conjures up an image of juicy ripeness for me and implies that one is abundantly available for living. As long as 'fat' is used as a descriptive term, rather than a judgment or a weapon against me, I'm fine with that definition."

Lisa, a twenty-nine-year-old aerobics instructor, utterly rejects being referred to as "obese." She said, "The term 'obese' sounds like 'oh beast' to me. I find it totally offensive. So whenever I hear that word used, whether applied to me or not, I express my negative reaction by making funny sounds. I growl, roar, and hiss like a beast. People get the point, usually smile with me, and understand how that might feel." In her lighthearted way, Lisa has found an effective means to communicate that she is uncomfortable with the clinical, medical word. "I'm much more comfortable with phrases like 'women of size' or 'women of substance.' These have a positive overlay to them."

Andrea, a successful magazine editor at age forty-nine, does not want to be aggressive with her business associates, but she also feels uncomfortable with many of the terms used to describe people who are large. She said, "Whenever someone uses an unflattering term, I gently pair their word with the word 'large,' a term I'm comfortable with. I'm not pushy, just firm."

I define myself as a bountiful woman. To me, bountiful is a way of life—full, rich, robust. While "overweight," "obese," and "fat" women may wait for life to begin or hide until something imagined is different, bountiful women move forward, regardless of their relationship status, the amount of money in their bank account, or the number that comes up on the scale. Some bountiful women never set foot on the scale. They lead healthy lives, make reasonable food choices, and let their bodies take their natural shape.

A bountiful woman may decide to exercise. She may not. She may decide to lose weight. She may not. She may decide to date. She may not. She may decide to advance her career, or invest her time in volunteer work, or take a class in medieval history, or she may not. She never sells herself short nor limits her choices because of her size. A bountiful woman lives life in the moment, as fully as anyone else on the planet.

Judy, a thirty-seven-year-old social worker, is a bountiful woman—positive and upbeat in a comfortable, relaxed way. Starting most days looking and feeling great, you might even say she struts when she walks down the street. Judy told me, "I'll walk down the street humming some song that energizes me. I especially like singing 'Pretty Woman' because I am! Yes, I know the movie had a different theme, but I've made it my song. Even though no one else hears the words I'm singing in my head, everyone must get the message that I'm okay in the world. I'm okay with myself, and that includes all of me." Not that every day is all sunshine and smiles. Judy admits, "I'm like anyone else. There are some days when I'm in the pits. I pull my energy into myself and shield myself from whatever or whomever I encounter. I'm like a turtle on those days, with a shell that protects me. But before I know it, I'm feeling confident and capable again, and I'm out strutting my stuff."

Judy is not the only strutter I know. A therapist by profession, Lee loves to strut, and has been referred to as "bigger than life"! She is visible. When she is in your presence, you know it. She wears hats. She wears big silky flowers. She wears flowing clothes made of gorgeous, magnificent fabrics, always in colors to enhance her beauty. She wears high-heeled shoes. Her personal fashion style often garners compliments, such as "beautiful" and "gorgeous." She glows and has her say when she talks. Lee told me, "Granted, some people seem overwhelmed by my presence at times, but most get swept up in my energy. Since I enjoy and accept myself, other people feel encouraged to enjoy and accept themselves as well. I've turned my size into an asset."

Not all, or maybe even most, large women want to or could pull this off. Lee has her own way of enjoying life to the utmost. But we can all follow Lee's example by choosing to be alive right now. Lee has her style; you have yours. Strut your stuff in a way that feels right to you. Express your self-acceptance in the way you walk, talk, dress, and handle your relationships. Any other way, as Lee would say, is just no fun.

Secrets for Bountiful Living

Define, develop, and embrace all of you.

→

Identify which terms make you feel comfortable and which turn you off. Tell people what is okay for you and what is not. Don't presume that they will or should know what is right for you.

→

Let people know how you feel in a positive, yet firm manner, or in a lighthearted way.

→

Pair the words you would want to hear with the words other people use.

→

Commit to a full life of bounty, however you define that life.

→

Strut your stuff!

→

Pick a theme song and hum it as you go through your day.

→

Wear yellow socks or whatever else pleases you! Even a fifty-year-old bountiful woman can wear yellow socks!

→

Say to yourself, "I deserve to feel good about myself, and I won't accept anything less." Or as Dame Edith Sitwell said, "Why not be oneself? That is the whole secret of a successful appearance. If one is a greyhound, why try to look like a Pekinese?"

→

Having fun is part of the complete life. What would be enlivening for you: laughing a full laugh, out loud? Being silly? Skipping down the street? You decide.

→

Mirror, Mirror on the Wall

*She saw that her rounded stomach looked like
the goddess she had just viewed at a museum
opening; the curve of her hips was akin to the
womanly women's.* —JANEEN

Every woman, regardless of size, knows that she is judged by her appearance. Women's bodies are verbally and visually dissected. They are rated on a regular basis in private conversation, over the Internet, and in every form of media. Those of us who are larger than the social ideal receive the lowest marks of all. We have been taught to believe that it is impossible to be beautiful and bountiful at the same time.

But we must not allow our sense of worth to be decided by the judgments of others, and certainly not by cultural or time-bound concerns. To the contrary, we have the right to decide for ourselves what is beautiful and how we want to present ourselves.

This is a complicated process for many bountiful women. Janeen, a thirty-year-old nurse, is well acquainted with the different ways people look. While she treats every patient with the dignity she believes they deserve, she hasn't always given herself that same respect. She told me about a watershed moment that transformed her into a bountiful woman. She said, "While getting ready for my next shift, I emerged from the shower as I did every morning, but on this day, I caught sight of myself in the mirror. Most of the time, I do not actually see myself. I might look at my face while I put on lipstick or fix my hair, but I avoided looking at my body, especially when nude. To be honest, I have felt fat and ugly. I was confident in my profession and positive about other people's bodies, but negative, critical, and self-loathing about my own." Janeen knew she had been denying the changes in her body as she had gained weight. She had purchased new uniforms as she grew larger, but did not let herself actually acknowledge how she had changed.

This particular morning was different. Janeen did two things that created a significant shift for her. First, she made a list of all the things her body could do, and do well, at her current weight. She wrote, "I can be on my feet much of the day and still have energy for shopping in the evening. I can carry a fifty-pound bag of food for my dog into the house without being winded. I can manage my own luggage whenever I travel." She also listed medical assets that she had learned through her nursing training. She wrote, "Osteoporosis is a lesser risk for me because, as a large person, I strengthen my bones just by moving around the world."

The second thing she did was harder: she actually looked at her body without any clothes on. She asked herself, "What parts of my body do I like?" To her surprise, she found quite a few. She decided that she would allow herself to keep looking. She saw that her rounded stomach looked like those of the beautiful goddesses she had just viewed at a museum opening; the curve of her hips was akin to those womanly women's.

If a woman can't look at herself honestly and lovingly, her own self-rejection will clearly show. We might try to hide our bodies behind our clothing (or denial or other forms of camouflage), but we're fooling no one but ourselves. How we see ourselves without our clothing is revealed in how we present ourselves to the world.

While most women, if not most people, worry about their appearance, larger women often agonize over what to wear. Some put off buying new clothes until they reach the weight they want or at least until they're in the process of losing weight. Others try to avoid the issue altogether. Such was Carol, a veterinarian, who dressed casually for work. As she gained weight, Carol did not upgrade her wardrobe. She frequently pulled, tugged, struggled, and adjusted her clothes to get more comfortable in them. She never felt she looked attractive—that is, if she even let herself think about how she looked. Carol, while clearly a smart and well-educated person, did not accept her body; she had been torturing it, and it was apparent to everyone around her. In fact, Carol's bra was so tight that her skin bulged out over it and left unflattering lines.

One day, the dreaded happened—someone made a comment, albeit a comment intended to help, not insult, Carol.

Her good friend Annette, also bountiful, suggested they go shopping at an outlet that carried lower cost clothes for all sizes. Carol felt awful, put down, criticized. But Annette persisted, knowing there were options. She was not put off by Carol's sense of offense or embarrassment.

Carol told me, "Annette would not let me off the hook, even though I was upset with her for pointing out the obvious. She offered me catalogs, lists of stores, and lovingly talked to me about how to present myself best. Annette said, 'Let's do this together, support each other, and find a way to be the best we can be.' Those words mattered to me. I heard them, and felt loved. We discussed how I could create my own neat, comfortable, and attractive way of being in the world." Annette's gift of friendship was finding the right words that Carol could hear, while also offering her support, information, and a nudge in the right direction—even though Carol was initially prickly about the possibilities.

We all need support and feedback when we're sorting through our alternatives and creating our own way of expressing ourselves. Belinda, a fifty-eight-year-old English professor, felt best when her hair was cut, her clothes were right, and she was put together, but she no longer felt comfortable with her "look." She told me, "I was reluctant to go to a department store to experiment with new makeup because I didn't know what to expect or whether I'd get the help I needed. Often the chairs are so small, and I wanted to work with a woman who had a positive attitude toward larger women. After some thought, I realized that I was as entitled to feel good about my appearance as any other woman. I debated about going to a salon where they would give me a private lesson, but then decided against that because there would probably be more pressure to buy their products. I finally called a quality department store and made an appointment after talking to the woman who would work with me. I told her about my concerns, and she was delightful. When I went for my appointment, it was like meeting an old friend."

At sixty-two, Lena decided she also needed a new look. In her work as a tailor, she noticed that every large woman who came into her shop had essentially the same hairstyle—short on the sides and full, often curly, on the top. Lena said, "I looked at myself in the mirror and realized that I had the same cut, too. The next time I went to my hair salon, I realized that all of the large women getting their hair fixed had the same style going. I don't know if we all chose that look because it was easy to care for or if we all believed that the style was slimming to our faces or what. But I decided I wanted to create my own look." It took a little effort to find a hair stylist who wasn't stuck in the same rut. She said, "I had to look for a new person, someone who was able to offer me a range of options. It was worth the effort, though. I love my hair now. It's longer and I'm experimenting with different kinds of combs and headbands. I feel the best I have in years."

What you wear or don't wear, how your hair is styled or not styled, is not the issue; the point is to give yourself the opportunity to explore your attractiveness in a safe environment, knowing, deep in your being, that you have choices. That's the essence of being a bountiful woman. Rachel, at sixty-five, spoke of the years she spent limiting her own choices. She recalled, "I didn't want to accept the fact that I had gained as much weight as I had, so I'd buy things that were actually too small for me, hoping and planning to lose weight to fit into them. Of course that hardly ever happened. So eventually I had to throw out those items, never having worn them, or maybe having stuffed myself into them once or twice."

Now Rachel buys very loose clothes so they fit comfortably, whether she loses or gains weight. She likes tie-dyed dresses that are unrestrictive and comfortable. Rachel smiled, "I do most of my shopping from catalogs. I wore one of my favorite dresses to an outdoor theater where my daughter was performing. A young man came over and said, 'I just wanted to tell you that your dress is beautiful, and we've been looking at it throughout the whole performance.' The 'we' he was referring to was the band giving the show. What a compliment to have the entire band notice my dress! I got a kick out of that."

Renee, forty-five, enjoys the sensual feel of natural fibers—silks, linen, cashmere, and, recently, pashmina. She loves to shop and is no longer willing to frequent stores that are unfriendly to bountiful women and will not buy great outfits in sizes that are too small. She repeats to herself, "No more 'weighting' for me" whenever there is a choice to be made, as if it were a mantra.

Not every woman feels comfortable wearing makeup or putting much emphasis on trendy fashions. Some bountiful women exercise their options by developing a style that is uniquely, and more subtly, their own. Jennifer, at fifty-nine, describes herself as a "hippie of the '60s" who prefers a natural look and has little time or patience for putting on makeup or fussing with her hair. She said, "One of my close friends, Mickey, is the glamorous type who accentuates her beauty through the use of makeup and hip hairstyles. She was always after me to experiment with my appearance, not to please anyone else, but as an artistic expression.

"After a serious health scare, I thought, 'Why not?' It was time for some new experiences." She called Mickey to go with her on an adventure to the department store. She knew, of course, that this was an experiment and not a change in her value system. Like schoolgirls kicking up their heels and play-acting at dress-up, Mickey and Jennifer shopped, tried on clothes styles neither of them had ever worn, and experimented with different kinds of makeup. Jennifer enjoyed the play and the laughter, and liked some of the ways they added color to her face. Even though she was eventually content with her natural appearance, she had explored her look. She saw herself in a new way, and was all the more comfortable in her own personal style.

Sometimes it takes a tragic situation to help us reset our priorities and enjoy ourselves for the beauties we are. Such was the experience of Susan, a sixty-four-year-old wife of a physician. Even though both she and her husband, Jim, were somewhat large, Susan felt that she was judged harshly, while her husband was referred to as "a teddy bear." Often surrounded by sleek, svelte wives at social events, Susan thought that they were too often focused on their weight and critical of hers. The social pressure, along with finding out that her blood pressure was elevated, triggered a season of self-doubt and self-criticism.

In anticipation of attending a special dinner, Susan purchased a dark blue floor-length silk gown. Trying it on at the store, she thought it was elegant and flattering. She also purchased comfortable new undergarments that helped the dress fit just right. To complete the outfit, Susan bought new shoes and an exquisite bag with silk roses across the top. "All this planning," she told me, "was to make the evening a pleasure. However, the morning of the event, I woke up feeling bloated and puffy. I was grumpy all day, irritable with anything that did not go well. I put off getting ready.

"Then, fate took over. Our neighbor from across the street, Stan, came over and asked Jim for help, saying that his wife was not feeling well and he was worried. Jim went over to see her and recognized that she was having a heart attack. Jim called the paramedics, who took her to the hospital. That moment," Susan emphasized, "helped me put things into proper perspective. I felt like I was being told to live fully in the present, live with enthusiasm, live with energy. You never know how long you have on earth, and it's a waste of time to get bogged down in the things that don't matter. Once Jim checked in with the hospital and found out that our neighbor was doing well, I said, 'Honey, this is going to be a great evening. Let's celebrate every single moment together!"

Susan finished getting ready for the evening, savoring the sensuality of the silky dress, noticed how her skin looked next to the rich color, and felt beautiful as she and Jim went out the door—a shift into a sense of well-being she completely enjoyed. While denial, procrastination and irritability are frequent ways of coping with less than ideal parts of our lives, confronting our reality with a hopeful or positive outlook can make a tremendous difference. From head to toe, you have the right to feel good about your body and to express your beauty in your own particular style.

More Secrets for Bountiful Living

Buy clothes that fit, feel good, and are
enhancing to you. Torturing yourself in clothes
that do not fit does not build your character or
make you thinner; it just makes you feel terrible.

➔

If your weight changes, move those clothes
out of sight, or better yet, give them to someone
else who can enjoy them. If your weight and
body change, those styles may not work for
you anymore.

➔

Experiment with the possibilities of how you can
feel and look your best, however you define that
look. Let a friend whose appearance you admire
help you out. Do not accept the stereotyped view
of how you should look; find your own way.

➔

Savor your body and its sensuality,
all of its sensations, from the feel of the material
you wear to the aroma of your skin.

→

With a friend, make an outline of your body on
butcher block paper; write on it every single part
of your body that you can appreciate, similar to
what Janeen did by looking at herself in the
mirror. Let your friend add her perceptions, too.

→

Do a collage, or other art project,
acknowledging the beauty of bountiful women.

Pampering

*. . . I put a great deal of value in maintaining
my own center, honoring my own interior needs.
I nurture a deep connection with myself on a
spiritual level through meditation,
breathing, and walking.* —JUDY

If we're not taking care of ourselves in the same ways we take care of other people, all the verbal affirmations in the world can't mask our true feelings of self-rejection. Bountiful women need to treat their bodies with the respect and nurturing they deserve. Sandy, a forty-one-year-old businesswomen, knew about taking care of herself, although admittedly she did a better job some weeks than others. She told me about an early pampering experience. "With my weight, my feet and legs became easily tired, but I was reluctant to indulge myself in a pedicure. Thank god for good friends! My girlfriend gave me the nudge I needed by giving me a gift certificate for a manicure and pedicure.

"The manicure sounded good—I like to feel polished—but I'd never had a pedicure before and was not sure how it would be. Well let me tell you, it was amazing! It was so soothing, so positive, so comforting, so everything good. The woman who did the work sanded, smoothed, and moisturized my feet and legs." Sandy smiled as she talked about the experience.

By taking such good care of her legs and feet, Sandy felt grand at that moment. Best of all, when she went out the next day, her feet felt truly different. Where there had been calluses and roughness, smooth skin allowed her shoes to fit more comfortably. Her stockings did not catch, and she felt like she was walking on air.

Sandy acknowledged, "My next challenge was being brave enough to get a massage. I felt so self-conscious about being undressed and having my body touched by someone who might make a negative judgment about me. I found Carol, a massage therapist, with whom I immediately felt at ease. One thing that helped me was that we talked beforehand about massage—its therapeutic and psychological value. I could tell that she understood how tight and tired I had been feeling. Carol gave me the choice of wearing undergarments or being naked during the massage. She said I'd be covered with a sheet the entire time, so I'd never be 'exposed.' It was up to me, but I'd have a fuller massage if I were unclothed. With my courage intact, I decided to go for it. I took off all my clothing and slipped between the sheets. At first I was holding my breath, but before Carol returned to the massage room, I started breathing slowly in time with the soothing music."

Carol rubbed, pressed, pushed on pressure points, and before Sandy knew it, she was floating. The aches and pains melted away, leaving her feeling energized and soothed at the same time. Sandy said, "Not only did I feel better physically, I was emotionally nurtured by having someone touch me in such a safe, caring, and accepting way. I don't know why I waited so long. As soon as the massage was over, I scheduled another one for the following week. I'm determined to continue feeling as superb as I did at that moment." Feeling good in body and soul is something bountiful women experience on a regular basis, even if it means taking risks and trying out new experiences.

Linda, an interior designer, decided that she would treat herself to a fancy, glamorous spa resort for her fiftieth birthday. Learning was an important personal goal for Linda, and on this significant birthday, she wanted to be somewhere that would allow her to learn more about herself. Even though everyone pictured on the brochures (and everyone she imagined she would meet there) had thin, toned bodies, she felt she deserved to enjoy such a magnificent place.

Linda did her homework. She talked with her travel agent, went on the Internet, talked with other spa goers, found out what she wanted, and then contacted a spa directly. She told me, "I was very frank with them. I told them I was large and, to my delight, I was told that this particular spa had what they called a Life Enhancement Program—a subset of people in a separate area of the spa who received personal attention and opportunities to learn about health, fitness, nutrition, and managing stress. While this special program was a bit more expensive, I knew immediately that this was what I was looking for." In preparation for the trip, Linda bought comfortable exercise clothes and off she went.

She recalled, "It was fabulous! It was majestic! I was definitely the largest person there, but no one treated me any differently than anyone else. In fact, every single person I met was helpful and encouraging. At meals, I ate everything I wanted, and if the portions were too small for me, I'd ask for more. No one hassled me. Plus, I tried out watsu massage, shiatsu massage, reflexology, weight training, and even went on a long hike in the mountains. I didn't know I could walk that far, but since I was participating fully in the spa community, I knew I could ask for help if I needed it. I had the time of my life!" Linda's experience was joyful because she planned ahead, asked about her concerns, and was open to new opportunities. She added, "I could have limited myself by blaming my size, or even by assuming that other people would hinder me somehow. But instead, I got in there like everyone else. People were as flexible as I let them be."

I'm not suggesting that you have to take off to some tropical island for sand and sea to take good care of yourself. Bountiful women pamper themselves in expansive ways, and in small, everyday sorts of ways too. Take Judy, a forty-six-year-old psychologist, for example, who sees pampering herself as daily self-acceptance. Relaxed and unimpressed by airs, Judy dresses casually and comfortably, exuding an air of tranquility. She told me, "I've had people comment that they can hardly imagine me in an agitated state. That's because I put a great deal of value in maintaining my own center, honoring my own interior needs. I nurture a deep connection with myself on a spiritual level through meditation, breathing, and walking."

As a bountiful woman, Judy is determined to feel worthy. These self-caring activities (all free she reminds me) result in her being at ease and content with herself. She is present, calm, and peaceful. "I spoil myself," Judy told me proudly, "simply by being myself. I thrive in situations where I can comfortably be who I am." In addition to using various spiritual practices, Judy invests in relationships that are genuinely meaningful to her. She said, "I am drained by people who require a lot of attention, or who need to be the center of attention, or who insist that I fit their mold. One way I take care of myself is to avoid such people, or limit my time with them if they are, for some reason, unavoidable. But even when with people who clearly criticize my behavior, I insist on being me. For example, because of my size, I can't cross my legs, so I like to put them up whenever I'm sitting. So I do. I don't like wearing shoes, so I take them off whenever I can. I'm not one for pretense. What you see is what you get. I want to be with people who are accepting of me as I am, not how they need me to be."

Who can disagree with this logic? Feeling safe and nurtured on a daily basis is the best form of pampering. And asking for what you really want from friends and family can help bring more nurturing into your life.

I learned about another creative approach to pampering from Karen who celebrated her fortieth birthday by asking her friends to prepare meals for her and her family, rather than giving her gifts. At first everyone thought she was kidding, but she was asking for exactly what she wanted.

Karen described her busy life: "My husband and I have six children between us—two from my first marriage, two from his first marriage, and two of our own. Since I work nearly full-time, I was exhausted having to come home each day and cook for that huge brood. I'd say to myself, 'Gee I wish someone else was cooking dinner right now so I could put my feet up, or take a hot bath, or just sit on the couch and rest a few minutes.' I simply listened to myself and decided that that was what I wanted for my birthday."

When her friends asked her what to get her, she'd say she wanted meals made for her family—one meal, two meals, however many at any time. Her friends realized that she was serious and began signing up to provide those meals. Some brought candles and flowers and even stayed to do the dishes. Others dropped over simple meals that were unpretentious but delicious. Karen said, "Sometimes I got to pick what we would eat. It was a real breakthrough for me since I've often felt self-conscious about letting myself eat in front of other people, or even letting people know that I eat at all. This whole experience felt totally self-indulgent and I loved it. The great part was that I didn't get a pile of gifts I didn't really want. I had friends signed up to provide meals for us at least once a week for a year! Can you believe it? I felt so totally cared for and pampered every time someone showed up with something yummy."

Pampering can take all forms—from making sure to ask for an armless chair at a restaurant or in a waiting room, to having pantyhose that fit. Some ways of pampering yourself come at no cost, while others are high-ticket items. Regardless of the price tag, the goal of pampering is to feel spoiled, indulged, cherished, comforted, and accommodated—the way bountiful women (and everyone else) want to feel.

More Secrets for Bountiful Living

Open yourself up to the world of pampering;
you deserve it.

→

Be adventurous. Take risks in trying new
avenues of nurturing.

→

Manicures, pedicures, massages, facials,
herbal wraps, and more are for anyone who says
to herself, "I would (or might) enjoy that
experience." Remember: Spas are for
bountiful people, too.

→

Don't be caught unawares. Call ahead of time
to talk to the restaurant, dentist, cruise ship,
travel agent, and so on, so you will know what
to expect and can make all the necessary
arrangements for an experience just right for you.

→

*Each and every day find ways to
spoil yourself, and then actually do them.*

➔

*Pampering is mindfulness, focusing on, paying
attention to, and doing what would enrich
your day-to-day experience.*

➔

Section Two

Friends, Foes, and Family

Motherrrrrr! Daaaaad!

*He doesn't have to be perfect to let me know he
loves me deeply and cares about the quality of
our relationship.* —CHRISTINE

Who else shapes and impacts us as strongly as our parents
do? And if they don't approve of the choices we make, or criticize our bodies, we can be devastated. What are the best ways
to handle a critical parent?

Sometimes setting clear and strong boundaries is the most
effective way to deal with the problem of repetitive criticism.
Evelyn, now seventy-four, told her story. "You might say I was
ahead of my time. I became a physician back when women
just didn't attempt such things. I felt like a pioneer, in spirit
and in body. Even as a young girl, I was sturdy, strong, and
larger than others my age. Many people told me not to be
such a tomboy, but I never bought it."

Indeed, Evelyn blazed her own trail. She married an engineer early in life, had three children, and still saw patients
until her recent retirement. She recalled the moment when
she confronted her mother about criticizing her size, many

years ago. "When I was in medical school, my weight was rarely discussed openly, but I knew there were comments made behind my back. As the years passed, I grew large, larger, larger still. I could handle comments made by outsiders, but not from my parents, especially my mother, who was constantly pressuring me to diet.

"Then came the moment of truth. My mother commented on my size one time too many, and I quietly said, 'I love you for who and what you are. I want you to love me for who and what I am. If you can do that, we shall have many happy times together. If not, I have to stay away.'" Fortunately, that was the last discussion they ever had about her weight. Evelyn stated her feelings clearly, her mother heard, and life went on but was forever changed.

Gail, an at-home mom of fifty-one, also took the direct approach with her mother who was determined that she lose the weight she gained with each of her three pregnancies. "Mom brought up a new diet regime or exercise program in many, if not all conversations. It drove me crazy! When I was younger, I felt obligated to try her suggestions, but they didn't work for me. One day I realized that I dreaded seeing her, and I didn't want to lose our relationship. So I told her straight out, 'Mom, for the sake of our relationship, I only want to hear good things from you. Not one more word about my weight—*not one more word!*'"

Gail smiled, "I'd like to say that from that moment on my mother was the embodiment of support and acceptance, but she wasn't. She still gets on me about my weight from time to time, but not like before. And somehow, since I made my declaration, I can shrug off her so-called suggestions. If she really gets to me, I simply end the conversation. I feel a new sense of power and self-acceptance." Ginny, another bountiful woman, echoes this sentiment. "I make it clear to my family that my size is not up for discussion. I just don't go there with anyone, no how, no way." Sometimes our mothers hear us, sometimes they don't. But you'll never know if you don't take the risk and speak up. If you mean what you say, and you say what you need to say, it can make all the difference, and sometimes does.

Of course mothers aren't the only source of unkind comments. Fathers can also make their share of negative barbs. Christine, a seminar facilitator, had a close and loving relationship with her father, especially after her mother died. As her weight increased, however, so did his critical comments. She told me, "I finally sat down and talked to him about how his comments made me feel. I explained to him that I needed his support, not his negativity. He is much better now," she said, "though he occasionally backslides. To his credit, right after he says something critical, he catches himself and apologizes.

"The best part is that I know he listened to me and heard me. He doesn't have to be perfect to let me know he loves me deeply and cares about the quality of our relationship." Sometimes being straightforward, vulnerable, and honest is the best way to build solid relationships with our parents.

However, since not everyone is able to be straightforward, some bountiful women have trouble helping their parents "get it" and understand the impact of their comments on their children.

Such is the experience of Anne, a fifty-one-year-old psychotherapist. She's been various weights since the age of ten, each one critiqued by her perfectionistic parents. Anne told me, "The hardest thing for me has been dealing with my parents. I've spoken with them many, many times, telling them how much it hurts when they comment on my weight. I've given them things to read, tried being firm, ignored them, refused to speak to them for periods of time after having been clear about what I need. After all, I'm a therapist! I'm supposed to be good at communicating with people!"

After years of trying one approach after another, she stopped confronting them directly. "There are a few areas in our relationship where there is simply no agreement. Both sides are entrenched in our positions. They can't seem to stop trying to control me, and I'm absolutely opposed to them doing so. In spite of our tug-of-war over my weight, there is enough substance to our relationship that I'm willing to put up with it. In many ways, we have a very warm and happy relationship. I'm not interested in trying to be cruel to them, even though they are unintentionally cruel to me. I realize that I can't change them any more than they can change me. That helps me to see the dilemma. We each want the other to be what we want them to be."

In the final analysis, accepting others can be extremely difficult. While our parents often feel it is in our best interest to lose weight, we simply want to be accepted as we are—we want them to stop pressuring us, and they want us to follow their instructions. The acceptance that we long for from our parents may require that we begin by expanding our own ability to accept their foibles before they can accept ours, whether or not that seems fair. I'm not at all advocating that you allow your parents to damage your self-esteem or exert unhealthy control over your life. But if your efforts have been unsuccessful in the past, I suggest you try something different. When change is necessary, the challenge is who is going to go first. Often the person with the most discomfort is the one who must step up, or nothing will ever be different.

More Secrets for Bountiful Living

We need five positive interactions to every negative one to make a difference. Model for your parents how you want to be treated by showing and telling them how much they mean to you. Saying "Thank you," "I'm glad to see you," or "You taught me this or that while growing up," sets a tone for your interactions with them that may allow you to talk to them about other difficult topics. If they don't get the message, then be direct and tell your parents that you only want to hear pleasant things about yourself.

→

Don't take other people's reactions personally. Most people have their own reasons for what they say and do; it's almost always about them, not about you. (Even if their reaction is about you, you do not have to feel responsible for it.)

→

Confrontations often feel negative, or at least anxiety-producing, even if they ultimately have a positive outcome. Use them sparingly, and only when they are worth the price.

→

We can only change ourselves. As Anne said, "I realize that I can't change them any more than they can change me. That helps me to see the dilemma. We each want the other to be what we want them to be."

→

Sisters and Sisters-in-Law

Aunt Sylvia always said how beautiful I looked in the pictures I sent. She did not say, "You have such a pretty face, but . . ." and then fill in the blank with what was not good enough about me as so many other people did. —LONNIE

Competition and siblings are indelibly linked words. Beverly couldn't remember a time when she wasn't compared (negatively) to her sister, Jill. Beautiful, smart, and with a warm personality, everyone liked Jill. While Beverly was also quite bright, she never felt as attractive as her sister, a feeling that grew as her weight increased. Beverly told me, "Once we were grown and out of the house, my mom and Jill became even closer, ganging up on me about my size. It was like the two of them were on a mission to tell me how much better I'd look if I'd lose weight and dress differently. They even criticized my line of work, saying that computer programming wasn't something a woman should want to do. When the two of them got together, they could be ruthless, downright mean."

As a computer programmer living in Silicon Valley, Beverly fit right in with her jeans, T-shirts, running shoes, and hair pulled back casually. She continued, "The way I dressed was definitely not a look that appealed to my mother and Jill. I dealt with it by keeping my distance, seeing them only at holidays, while gritting my teeth."

And then, everything changed. Beverly became rich— extremely rich. She had been an early employee for a computer company that went public when Beverly was in her early thirties; she suddenly found herself a multimillion-airess. Now, at thirty-seven, she said, "All criticism abruptly stopped, and the requests for financial assistance came pouring in. I was suddenly popular with my sister and mother. Jill asked me to help her buy a new house. My mom wanted a new car. I was amazed at how nice they could be when they both wanted to be, and when they wanted something from me.

"What a battle I had inside! I've always seen myself as a generous person, and I had the desire to help the people I loved. However, all those years of harsh criticism soured my interest in helping Jill and Mom. I talked about it in therapy and decided that I didn't feel comfortable making any financial decisions until we cleared the air."

Beverly set up a meeting with her sister and mother and attempted to talk about the past. Neither one was open to the discussion. Instead, they both acted like they didn't know what Beverly was talking about, denying that they had ever been critical of her appearance or professional choices. It was an extremely discouraging conversation.

Beverly told me, "I felt incredibly angry at their denial of the hurt they had inflicted. At that moment, I gave up hoping that the three of us could ever be close, a painful and sorrowful realization for me.

"After a lot of thought, soul-searching, and counseling, I acknowledged that I did not want to give them money for luxuries. It was hard to admit, because I want to see myself as a giving person, but that's how I honestly felt. Instead, I set up a college fund for Jill's children and another fund for my mother to be used in the event that she had serious medical problems. I can live with myself knowing that I've helped my family, but I've not allowed them to take advantage of me. I feel very good about these decisions. Of course, I still have moments when I wish it were different. Mostly, though, I just see it for what it is."

Feeling good about oneself can be a challenge where jealousy abounds, as Galen, sixty-nine, knows. She told me, "It took a long time for me to admit that whenever I spent time with my sister, Helen, I'd be depressed and exhausted for days. I felt awful. I'd always blame some bug that was going around. Eventually, though, I had to face the fact that what she said and did undermined my confidence.

"If you saw us together, you might think that I'd be the jealous one, rather than the other way around. She can eat anything she wants and never gain weight. I *look* at a piece of cake and grow larger. Men are drawn to her wherever she goes. In fact, she's been married three times. I've been married for many years to the same man, and perhaps that's part of the problem. Helen thinks that she deserves to be the one with the solid, happy marriage. After all, I'm heavy and she sees herself as more attractive.

"Even though I didn't want to face her jealousy for a long time, I found myself putting myself down in front of her and telling her what a great life she had. I'd say how pretty she was, you know, anything that would make her life sound better than mine. She'd always respond with some snide remark about my weight. This went on for years."

Finally Galen had had enough. Having grown in her self-acceptance, she wasn't willing to go through this defeating dance any longer. Galen stopped putting herself down, and whenever her sister commented on her weight, Galen asked her not to speak to her that way. Helen was taken aback at first, and then spent much less time with Galen. Galen told me, "I miss seeing her as much as before, but I don't miss the dismissive comments and the depressive aftermath of our visits. If she can't treat me with respect, then I'll forgo the so-called sisterly get-togethers."

For our own sakes, it may be better to stop trying and start telling the truth about the relationship. Such was the situation with forty-five-year-old Diane, who has a twin sister, Darla. With the biological connection, Diane always hoped that she and her sister could be there for each other. Diane was larger than Darla, yet Darla always said that Diane was beautiful and that her extra pounds did not detract from her appearance. Even though the words sounded supportive, something put Diane off balance. She blamed herself for being suspicious, but received clarity on their fortieth birthday.

Diane and Darla planned a joint birthday dinner at a local Japanese restaurant. Everyone arrived, took their places at the table, and then Diane realized that Darla was monitoring her every word, her every bite, her every everything, and, like a sportscaster, was giving continual commentary. Darla's comments sounded so helpful, so encouraging, so enlightening, but there were so many, so incredibly many, of them. Diane told me, "Darla said things like, 'Are you comfortable in that space? Maybe you're too cramped and need more room,' or 'Maybe you've had enough. Let's have the server clear the table,' or 'Oh, that piece of birthday cake is too big for Diane. Here, give her this smaller one.' I realized that her attentiveness was actually a strange way to control me. By allowing her to 'take care of me,' I was allowing my confidence to be undermined."

Later, Diane met with Darla and described how the evening felt to her. Darla was defensive at first, but then she was able to see how her comments impacted Diane. To her credit, when Darla recognized her unconscious pattern of relating, she stopped. Both sisters can feel proud of the way they handled their relationship—Diane for risking honesty and Darla for having the strength of character to acknowledge and change her behavior.

Bountiful living often requires courage and the willingness to grow from our mistakes. Being brave may mean continuing to speak up—or it may mean walking away if the other person will not honor you. Seeking a range of choices is a bountiful way of life.

Janice, in her forties, also had to stand up for herself in relationship to her critical sister. An executive with a major investment firm, Janice had a good life that she had worked hard to achieve. In the business world, Janice had to overcome the expectations people had for the appearance of a successful investment broker. And she did.

In contrast, Janice's sister, Ilene, had endless difficulties in her career, even though she was "the pretty one and the smart one," the one whom everyone expected to be wildly successful. It seemed that her sister always required their interactions to be focused on her. If Ilene asked Janice how she was doing at work, she would not listen to the answer. No matter what they talked about, the attention was always drawn back to Ilene. Janice never felt like she got her turn.

After one particularly demanding visit, Janice went home and wrote a poem that helped her release feelings of anger, disappointment, and nonacceptance. She said, "I didn't want to carry these feelings around with me anymore, so I wrote a poem entitled, 'You probably think this is about you.' The poem captured the endless experiences that were so draining for me. I felt so much better after being clear and honest, at least with myself, about what it was like to have such a sister.

Now I do not feel so agitated, angry, and annoyed. The writing helped to clarify what was in my mind and my heart." Like Janice, sometimes we try to make a relationship safe enough for us even when it can never be exactly what we want.

Sometimes our relationships with sisters-in-law can be just as challenging as those with our own sisters. Elizabeth, now thirty-eight, is in her second marriage to a man with a close extended family—parents, three brothers, their wives, and children. Eager to get along well with her new in-laws, she accompanied her husband to quite a few family get-togethers. Through her indirect comments about food, Elizabeth became aware that one of the wives was uncomfortable with Elizabeth's weight. For example, when they were out to dinner, her sister-in-law would pick at her food and point out how much fat was in every dish. Elizabeth felt that these comments were actually directed at her.

In addition, Elizabeth was disturbed when she heard this woman speak to her eight-year-old daughter about getting fat, telling her what to eat and what not to eat. Elizabeth's childhood was filled with encounters like this—where excessive focus was placed on her eating. She identified with this woman's daughter, and was concerned on her behalf.

Elizabeth told me, "My instinct was to stay as far away from my sister-in-law as possible. I simply wanted to avoid being in the position of feeling judged, as well as being irritated with the way she treated her daughter. But I knew that my husband was close to his family and that my withdrawing would cause tension in our marriage. So I decided to go toward the problem rather than away from it.

"I spent more and more time with my in-laws, being warm and nondefensive. Two surprising things happened. First, I got to know my sister-in-law much better and soon her comments about food diminished as we discovered a variety of common interests. We actually became fairly good friends. Second, because of our growing friendship, I was able to tell her about my experience as a child, how my parents obsessed about my eating. She listened as I urged her to let her daughter learn how to choose food for herself, rather than be forced to eat what pleased her mother. I told her that her daughter deserved the chance to get in touch with her own body's experience, which was what I wished my parents had done for me. She still gets after her daughter for eating certain things, but it seems to me that she really listened to my concerns. I think that her growing affection for me has softened her, sensitized her to commenting about weight and food. I'm glad I made the effort rather than assume that she and I could never be friends."

Making a special effort can be well worth the risk. Family members can become friends and allies, as Lonnie, a fifty-four-year-old associate for an automobile association, recalled. Because Lonnie's mother was self-righteous in her belief that being thin was morally superior, Lonnie looked to other female family members for support. Through her relationship with her Aunt Sylvia, married to her mother's brother, Lonnie was able to become more accepting of herself.

Aunt Sylvia, Lonnie's mother's best friend, was a gem. Not a skinny-minny herself, Sylvia always had a loving word for others, and was willing to be present and share her thoughts and feelings with Lonnie. Lonnie told me, "Aunt Sylvia always said how beautiful I looked in the pictures I sent. She did not say, 'You have such a pretty face, but . . .' and then fill in the blank with what was not good enough about me as so many other people did."

Lonnie realized that she had family members and friends who truly accepted her. The sadness that pervaded her feelings about her family were mitigated by her accepting the fact that some people feel one way and others feel another way. Yes she wished that her parents were willing to love her for who she was, but that was not to be. She found love in other places—especially in her Aunt Sylvia.

Lonnie discovered an unexpected side benefit as she spent more and more time with Aunt Sylvia—Lonnie began to feel an increased gentleness toward her own mother. Being around Sylvia opened up her heart and reminded her that not everyone felt the way her mother did. In addition she was increasingly able to see other sides of her mother. Yes her mother was critical about her body, but her mother also was fun and funny and insightful and worldly. In getting to know her mother through her aunt's eyes, Lonnie found value in her, rather than focusing solely on insulting things her mother said. She accepted both sides of her mother, who was, after all, a person with flaws and assets like everyone else.

While we may desire close family ties, some sisters (and sisters-in-law) are easier to relate to than others; some listen and some do not. Whether you decide to confront, withdraw from, or embrace the situation, insisting on safety in family encounters is an important part of living bountifully.

More Secrets for Bountiful Living

Give yourself permission to get support from a
therapist to sort through family dynamics.

→

Acknowledge how you really feel, not how you
think others want you to feel or how you think
you ought to feel. Choose whether or not to risk
honesty with the other people involved.

→

For a solution to a conflict or difficulty, try doing
something that is absolutely opposite from
what you have tried. A new direction is often
what is needed. See who is there for you, as
opposed to seeing who is not.

→

Understand that if you judge others, you may
be wasting your time. Look for what is missing
or underdeveloped in you own life, as with
Darla and Diane.

→

Home for the Holidays

*I decided it was more important to me to
be surrounded by love than to be self-involved
and worry about what anyone else thought.
I have the body I have.* —WANDA

If family relations are stressful, some of us simply keep our distance—but what about the holidays when the pressure is on to show up with a casserole and a smile? Paula, a fifty-six-year-old cartoonist, came from what she called, "a large Italian family with large opinions about everything, which they are happy to share, like it or not." For Paula, Thanksgiving was a "hellacious" annual event because she and her mother had had considerable conflict about her weight. She said, "My mother has to be right about everything, and my father goes along with her to keep the peace. I've spent years trying to deal with her declarations of truth relating to every aspect of my life, especially my weight. I dread Thanksgiving the most because my mother won't allow anyone else to help her. She's overwhelmed and exhausted, the house is crowded, and she doesn't want me to eat anything."

Last year I decided I was going to find a way to make Thanksgiving work for me. First, I took my friend Sherry along with me for moral support and a reality check. Sherry is every mother's dream—charming, outgoing, an outstanding listener, and she loves to eat. Exactly what an Italian family needs. Second, I developed a mental game plan for dealing with my mother's negative comments: I'd detach myself from anything she said, respond pleasantly, and then turn to Sherry for my needed support. My ultimate goal was not to be goaded into a confrontation with my mother. So off Sherry and I went.

"I had warned Sherry about what to expect. When my mother opened the front door, she greeted Sherry and then said to me, 'I hope you have something nicer than that to wear to Thanksgiving dinner.' Catching my breath, I said, 'I do, Mom. I'm glad to be here.'

"Thanksgiving wasn't picture perfect, with my mother and I enjoying an idyllic relationship, but with Sherry's help, I was able to deal effectively with everything that happened. In the past, I would leave upset and resentful. This year, I walked out triumphant. On the way home, Sherry and I howled over the amazing things my mother had said. Having someone there who could affirm my reality was so helpful. I wish things could be different with my mom, but at least I'm no longer caught up in her manipulations. I could still be there and enjoy what there was for me to savor." Taking this step helped Paula confront something that she had been try-ing to avoid for years—recognizing that it wasn't safe for her to be as close to her mother as she wished. It was disappointing for her, but keeping her balance and dignity was much more important.

Paula is one of many bountiful women who dread Thanksgiving. Alice, a forty-nine-year-old publisher, is sometimes described as brave and courageous, "where angels fear to tread, there goes Alice." Nothing scares Alice—except maybe an invitation to a family Thanksgiving. She told me, "I decided to tackle this problem head-on. I went to therapy, talked to friends, cried a lot, felt anger, joined the size acceptance movement, read everything I could find, had massages so my body could feel touched with care, love, respect, and tenderness—anything and everything to find more comfort with and for myself.

"Then came the big test—the holidays. Last Thanksgiving there were thirty relatives gathered together, each one with their own expectations for me and each other, too. I decided not to behave as I had in the past, aware of and responsive to what I 'should' do. Instead, I did what I wanted to." Alice talked to those relatives she found of interest and didn't socialize with those she preferred to avoid. She decided to let them see who she really is, since she knows she can pretend to be so many different things.

With a solid sense of herself, Alice explained, "I can be sweet, funny, smart, caring, assertive, quiet, the life of the party, and in each of those modes, I can be comfortable with myself. What a delight to discover that I was no longer dependent on some relatives' reactions and responses—I was being guided by what was inside of me." Alice gave herself the encouragement she needed to be present with the various aspects of herself. She said, "While this may sound Californian, I summoned up all the energy of the universe, all the energy of my friends, dead and alive, to support me, encourage me, remind me of the beauty they saw in me, and the joy that is me. In my mind, I slowly looked at their faces as they regarded me with love, care, and joy. Their faces, their energy, allowed me to just be myself. I had the best trip ever."

After the Thanksgiving dinner is digested, many of us focus our attention on the next challenge—Christmas or Chanukkah. Each family has its own traditions, some endearing, others laden with obligation and trepidation. Something as simple as gift selection can become tricky for some bountiful women.

Twenty-two-year-old Ellen, a university student, told me about the complexity of dealing with Christmas gifts in her family. "Everyone makes a list of what they want complete with sizes, colors, and any other details. The family tradition is to give clothes as the main gifts. I don't like to give out my sizes. In fact, I barely know what size I wear at any given moment because my weight has varied so much over the years. Regardless, I definitely do not want to post a size list on the family website! Besides, I have my own style of dress and my family's choices often miss the mark." What to do? She said, "I wasn't particularly interested in making waves or creating a scene with my family, but I was determined to find a way to enjoy the holiday."

Ellen, creative and inventive, gave a list of stores and catalogs that carry items she likes, and asked for gift certificates. In another burst of resourcefulness, she chose some fancy, more expensive items that she could never buy for herself. She specifically asked for a cashmere cape, a silk scarf, and some jewelry, none of which required giving a size, but were still generally clothing related. Her family had never exchanged luxurious items before. "What a difference this has made for me! I actually looked forward to the family gift exchange! Definitely this was the best Christmas I've had since I was a kid. The next year several other people added fancy items to their lists."

Traditional family holidays pose myriad challenges to bountiful women—but some of the "smaller" holiday celebrations can also become problematic. Even holidays like the Fourth of July have their own complexity. At sixty-four, Wanda, a government worker, was married with four grown children all living in the same town—a town that sponsored a big Fourth of July celebration every summer. As picture-perfect as a Rockwell painting, Wanda's small town did it all— the picnic, the three-legged races, the hats, the music, all of it.

Wanda had enjoyed the festivities as her children were growing up. They went every year and did all there was to do, including participating in the bake sale to raise money for the local Girl Scout troops. However, as she got older and larger, she was increasingly uncomfortable with deciding what to wear, had a difficult time sitting at those hard picnic tables with attached benches that were often too close for comfort, and sometimes she was hesitant to actually eat what she wanted. She did not find the experience as good as she remembered and wanted it to be. Perhaps she could have quietly withdrawn from the festivities, had it not been for the fact that she had taught her children to enjoy the holiday, and they wanted to pass the tradition on to their children.

She groaned as she recounted, "A few years ago, my oldest daughter, a consummate organizer I might add, came up with the idea that everyone in the family should dress in some way to identify us as family—all of us—our four children, their partners, all the in-laws, and the seven grandchildren. She decided that we'd all wear red shorts, white tops, and these blue caps that my daughter was going to have printed. Everyone thought it was nifty that this entire family got along and wanted to be together. Except for me. Of course I was happy about the family, but I did not want to wear red shorts. I had not worn shorts of any color in years. I didn't even know where to find red shorts in my size, let alone imagine how I'd look in them! Ugh!"

Wanda plunged into the usual round of self-recriminating thoughts, next tried to encourage herself, then decided she couldn't do it and looked for a way out of it. She grinned as she said, "I stopped and looked at the situation from a different direction. I realized that my daughter was trying to celebrate family, not embarrass me; her plans, which I was finding so hard to handle, were not at all about me. They had nothing to do with my size. That was my issue. I decided it was more important to me to be surrounded by love than to be self-involved and worry about what anyone else thought. I have the body I have. I have given birth and life to this family, and that family is proud to be recognized as a loving unit. So I made the effort and showed up with my shorts, just like everyone else in my family."

Yes, there were moments of discomfort, but paying attention to what truly mattered to her, getting focused on the significance of the event, being open and receptive to the love with which she was surrounded, made every moment of that day important to Wanda. The family took lots and lots of pictures, which she saved and treasures. "Even though," she groans, "there are many photos of me in those red shorts." Sometimes going with the flow is the fullest way to experience life.

Another bountiful woman, Eve, a thirty-two-year-old homemaker, also discovered that embracing the moment adds more joy than avoiding a celebration. Halloween is Eve's favorite holiday and has been since she was a child. She loved playing dress up as a child and enjoyed the family costume box that was always available for play. Her father was involved with community theater, and he often asked his daughter to read lines with him. As an adult, Eve retains her childlike enjoyment of life, and can be silly and outrageous at times, sexy and alluring at other times. As her size increased, she was hesitant about being so visible as she planned her Halloween costume, yet her great pleasure in the holiday overrode those hesitations.

"Last year," she recalled, "as Labor Day approached, I did what I always did, I thought about Halloween. As soon as summer is over, I look to the fall with anticipation. My next-door neighbors decided to have a party. I wondered whether I should go for camouflage, exaggeration, or just have fun. After more obsessing than I want to admit, I knew I had to do what I had to do."

Any guesses on her costume? Believe it or not, she went to that party as a frog, wearing all green, and she had a great time hopping around and croaking. She had a grand time and so did her husband and everyone else. Now you may or may not see yourself becoming a frog, but what do you have to lose by abandoning yourself to the simple silliness of Halloween or other playful occasions? You might wear a green, bushy wig or go glamorous and wear long eyelashes with a low-cut sweater to be a Marilyn look-alike. Much of the joy is in the possibilities.

Holidays are charged with history and expectations. Finding the right combination of self-care, attention to others, and enjoyment, is the goal. Much of our success comes from anticipating, planning, and then doing whatever it is we need to do to truly enjoy the holiday season. After all, holidays are a time for everyone.

More Secrets for Bountiful Living

Bring a friend along when visiting with family—
someone who can act as a buffer between you
and difficult relatives and can help you debrief
after the holiday.

→

Refuse to focus on the downside of an event and
avoid "catastrophic" thinking. Accept your
family situation as it is, whatever it is.

→

Lighten up. So what; if you're large, you're large.
You know it. They know it. Relax and make a
point to enjoy yourself. Maybe even play and
have fun. Why does your size have to be such
a big deal?

→

Say to yourself, "I am going to make this work
for me." Holidays and vacations are
your time, too.

→

*Remember, forgiveness does not necessarily
mean forgetting or absolving people for what
they have done; forgiveness is feeling peaceful
yourself. Feelings are energy. Let that energy
move you forward in bountiful ways.*

→

Friends Who Mean Well

*At first, Ginny didn't like the "new me," but I
realized that this important relationship had
become a testing ground for a new way of being.
. . . It was about whether or not it was okay
for me to be my size.* —CAROLYN

Our friends want the best for us. After all, isn't that one of
the distinctions of being a good friend?

The difficulty comes when our friends want one thing for
us, and we want another. Some of our friends may believe
that what is best for us is to be thin, while we want to be
accepted as we are. Such was the case with Ginny who really
worried about how much weight her friend Carolyn was carrying. Ginny said, "I didn't talk much about it, but I was
afraid for Carolyn because she was so large. I love her and
didn't want her to suffer from the health problems that sometimes go along with weight. I didn't understand why Carolyn
didn't simply lose weight."

Carolyn continued the story, "It all came to a head one
afternoon when we were cohosting a party. Ginny and I both
love to cook, explore new recipes, and share these discoveries

with friends. We'd been cooking together for years, but I tried to hide the fact that I needed to taste the food as I was cooking to make sure the dish was coming out right. I felt that Ginny did not approve of my tasting, seeing that as contributing to my weight. I would either sneak a taste when she wasn't looking, or actually cook the dish before we got together so she'd never know. Every time I tasted something while cooking, I'd hear Ginny's critical voice in my head." Carolyn and Ginny can laugh now about that particular afternoon.

Ginny smiled, "Out of the blue, Carolyn announced with a great deal of passion, 'I *must* taste these dishes while I cook and I'm fed up with your criticism!" Ginny just stood there, not grasping what Carolyn was saying or why she was so upset. Carolyn admitted, "I was just learning how to voice my feelings, and I came on way too strong. Resentment had built up in me, and I released most of it in one explosive episode.

"At first, Ginny didn't like the 'new me,' but I realized that this important relationship had become a testing ground for a new way of being. It wasn't simply about whether or not I tasted food while cooking; it was about whether or not it was okay for me to be my size. We had some rough times because the issues got all mixed up, and sometimes I said things too strongly and Ginny reacted, both to what I was saying and to how I was saying them.

"But Ginny is really important to me, and I to her. So we persevered. After some good counseling and support, I was able to talk to Ginny about the way I was accepting myself, just as I was, without losing weight. We even had several counseling sessions together."

Ginny added, "I thought couple's therapy was just for romantic couples, but I was glad when Carolyn suggested we try this. I'm so grateful that she cared enough about our friendship to put her feelings out on the table. I just didn't know how to put my concerns and feelings into words, and when I tried, Carolyn felt judged and rejected. Now we can both say how we feel, and hear what it's like for the other. I doubt that we would have made it on our own, without the help of therapy." What a loving gift these women have given to each other. Do whatever it takes to salvage a valuable friendship—go to workshops, read excellent books, benefit from individual or group psychotherapy, and take the risk of being honest with each other.

Even though I advocate talking openly with your friends, an honest exchange might not always work out the way we hope. Lee, a fifty-two-year-old psychologist, had issues with a friend of hers named Ann, who felt jealous of Lee. Lee told me, "Ann is a literary agent and successful in her own right, yet she had trouble with all I've been able to accomplish in my career. She would comment that people liked me because I was heavy, or that I received an award, not because I'd worked for it, but because my appearance drew people to me. It was a flaw that made me seem more accessible. Ann actually believed that the success I enjoyed came to me because of my size. I wasn't 'perfect' so people could be more comfortable with me, I suppose." Jealousy can be a destructive force, distorting one's ability to see clearly. Ann's jealousy certainly altered her ability to see that Lee was a talented, hardworking, creative woman who contributed enthusiastically to her community. Ann's undermining comments robbed the two women of the chance to enjoy their relationship.

Lee continued, "I really wanted this friendship to continue, but not on these terms. I sat down with her and said, 'People say to me, "You're so talented, what can't you do?" and I'd answer, "I can't be thin." When I say that, somehow people see my humanity, my vulnerability. But my size does not make it easier for me to be successful, nor does it detract from my accomplishments. Simply, my size is not a problem or an asset for me. I will not allow you to use it as an explanation for my achievements or as a weapon to hurt me.'"

Sadly, this confrontation was more than Ann was ready to receive. Some friendships can't withstand a renegotiation of terms, and the relationship falters and even dies as was the case with Lee and Ann. The people in our lives may not always be on our timetable, and may feel disquieted by how we change, grow, and express ourselves. When we change, or those we love change, everyone has to make adjustments. For a good friendship to survive, both women must adjust to those changes and be willing and able to have honest communication about their experience.

Fortunately, many friendships do adjust and even grow stronger due to change and confrontation. Linda, another bountiful woman told me how she and her close friend, Lenore, grew closer even though they now live far apart. They met while living in the same town, became good friends, and talked with each other about a variety of concerns, including the fact that they both struggled with their weight. Then Lenore moved away and they were no longer in daily communication.

A few months after Lenore moved, she returned to visit Linda. Delighted to see her good friend, Linda waited at a coffee shop with eager anticipation. Lenore appeared at the door, and immediately Linda noticed that she had lost a lot of weight. Linda hugged her, smiled, and spontaneously said, "You look so thin, so good!" Linda imagined that Lenore would take that comment as a compliment.

Both women sat down and Lenore quietly repeated the words that Linda had said—"You look so thin, so good." Linda, to her credit, got it right away. There had been an implied judgment in her comment that perhaps Lenore had not been okay before. Linda took a deep breath and said with a grin, "Hey, Lenore, you look so good!" Period.

Negativity slips easily into our language, even when our intention is to compliment each other. And not only "thin" people fall into this trap. Bountiful women do as well, because the correlation between looking good and being thin is so deeply ingrained in this society. While not every woman would have the same reaction Lenore did, many would, and do. Thankfully, Lenore gently confronted Linda, who in turn took responsibility for her comment. Even though geographical distance separates these two women, their hearts are connected more strongly than ever.

Our friendships with women can be the most stable, supportive, and nourishing bonds we will ever form. A friendship that endures, year in and year out, metabolizing the many changes that occur in the lives of both women, is a relationship grounded in honest communication.

Telling each other the truth, however, is not always easy. If there comes a time when your bond to another woman becomes unsafe for open exchange, no matter how long you've known each other, or how important you've been to each other in the past, you may have to let her go. After a time of grieving, you'll have room for new friendships that have the flexibility you need.

No one enjoys losing a friend, so I encourage you to do everything possible to salvage a relationship, even if it means getting professional assistance. Once we have navigated troubled waters together, our friendships can deepen and strengthen—results that are well worth the effort required.

More Secrets for Bountiful Living

Make room in your heart and mind for your
friends' differing and evolving opinions, feelings,
or ways of being.

➔

Be mindful of ways you discredit yourself or
others because of size.

➔

If you and a friend hit an impasse, don't be
reluctant to consult a therapist. A good
friendship is a treasure; it may be worth having
a few sessions to help you work through
the rough spots.

➔

Be willing to let go of a friendship that no longer
works for you. It may take some time to grieve
the loss, but in the long run, you will have made
the best decision for yourself and created the
space for someone new.

➔

Accepting Friends of All Shapes and Sizes

*As would be true of anyone with good
self-esteem, matching personality, interests,
knowledge, and friendliness are certainly more
important than any number on a scale.*

Bountiful women need and deserve external mirrors that reflect back acceptance and support. We may be required to put effort into cultivating relationships with other women who acknowledge our living bountifully. This is not to say that friendships should be based on size. I don't advocate discrimination in reverse, rather that you pick your friends wisely, without a sense of desperation or neediness. There are multitudes of women with whom you can bond. As would be true of anyone with good self-esteem, matching personality, interests, knowledge, and friendliness are certainly more important than any number on a scale.

Some women find themselves in need of new friendships as a result of their personal growth. Thirty-four-year-old Kathleen, a computer wiz who works in Silicon Valley, has invested an incredible number of hours into her career. She has worked, worked, and worked for years until she has skills, talents, and a successful career portfolio.

One day Kathleen took stock of her life and realized how isolated she had become, both socially and personally. She knew people at work and they socialized occasionally, even having dinner or drinks after work, but Kathleen did not have any close girlfriends to be with outside of work. In addition, she had gained weight over the years and as her body changed and her work pace increased, she had gradually pulled away from the women she had known. Her weight felt like an issue to her, although she was not totally clear whether it was an issue to other people.

She admitted, "Here I was, a successful 'sales techie,' not knowing how to meet women with whom I could build friendships. I wanted to find other women of size, like-minded women, who were living full lives. I approached the question the way I approached questions at my work. I went on a research mission!"

At the department stores and boutiques where she shopped for clothes, Kathleen found magazines, such as *Radiance* and *Mode*, which address larger women. She combed through the advertisements, finding an array of possibilities in her community. Before long, she was off to a gym called Women of Substance Health Spa, which describes itself as "the health club for women of all sizes, body types, and fitness levels . . . because the measure of a woman has nothing to do with numbers!"

Kathleen remembered, "I was overcome when I walked into that gym and saw all the classes, all the social events, all the people of all sizes doing healthy, invigorating things. On my first day, as I walked slowly on the treadmill, I began talking to a woman on the next machine. It turned out that we were both in sales, single, and in our thirties. We went out for dinner after our workout." Now, four years later, Kathleen and her "new" friend are part of a start-up company, hoping for an IPO, and, along with some other women of substance, have a supportive social network. Kathleen went on a quest to find like-minded people with whom she could feel comfortable in the body she had. She did a great job and found some lasting connections that gave her the friendships she was craving.

Other bountiful women maintain their long-term friendships through the changes that occur in life. Sue, a fifty-three-year-old wife, mother, and attorney, is the kind of woman who does everything well. Before taking a few years off to be with her children, she had been a partner in her firm, working long hours and receiving accolades and awards throughout her career. She has created a gorgeous home, is beautifully groomed and well-mannered, and has friends, healthy children, and a close relationship with her husband of twenty-seven years. Sue has a quietness about her that pulls you into her life. The words she uses to describe herself are plush, comfortable, round, and womanly.

You might think she has it all. And maybe she does, because she has also been part of a group of women, large and otherwise, who have supported each other emotionally over the years. The group, originally formed in the 1970s to focus on consciousness-raising, has changed, with people coming and going. Regardless, they meet every month. Sue described the group: "Some months, we have three people there; other months, there have been twenty. Some women have brought their daughters, daughters-in-law, neighbors, or friends. Over the years, I've been thinner and larger. Each person in the group has been different weights, some larger than others. We give each person five minutes to check in about whatever is on their mind, and then after everyone has had a chance to talk, the discussion is open. If all the time is used with check-ins, so be it. If not, the discussions are far reaching. Frequently, some woman is losing weight or gaining weight, which has become a topic of discussion.

"The values around having a positive image of your body, at whatever size, taking care of your health, moving, doing whatever you need to do to be alive, has permeated the group. No one is sure how that attitude emerged, but it has been a source of such constancy and such meaning that my life has been profoundly influenced by these associations, more than any other single factor in my life." Sue feels fortunate that this group has survived all these years. "Yet," she said, "if this group collapsed for whatever reason, I would go about gathering a new one."

Fifty-five-year-old Betty did take such a lead after losing her husband of thirty years to pancreatic cancer four years ago. She said, "I'd been married so long that I didn't know how to be in the world as a single woman, and my size made me more reluctant to 'get out there' as they say." But Betty did not feel good about being alone so much. She decided that she needed to be with other people. Another day alone in her house waiting for her grown children to call or for a friend to come by was only going to make her feel worse.

Betty told me, "After grieving the loss of my husband with the help of my therapist, I was ready to have a full life again. I looked in the local paper and in the telephone book trying to find a place where other large women might be. While I had not worked in years, I have an MBA and I knew there had to be a place for me, a place where I could feel comfortable. I went to the department store that sold large sizes and looked for flyers about any activities, to the library where I found books and magazines, to the Internet, but I could not find what I was after. So I decided that I was going to become a resource person for large women who wanted to meet each other and bond together to figure out life's challenges."

She put an ad in the local paper, calling for a hundred bountiful women to support and encourage each other. To her delight, within six weeks she had heard from sixty-one women; within three months the list was up to one hundred and ten. Betty smiled, "I've never felt better, more needed, more involved, more connected. I'm planning activities, a support group, lectures, and other gatherings."

Granted, not everyone is an organizational go-getter like Betty, but anyone can start a small support group with two or more other people. Invite a few girlfriends over for tea. Someone has to take that first step and say, "Let's get together."

More Secrets for Bountiful Living

*Finding other people to be with is good for
your emotional, psychological, and physical
health. Resist the urge to isolate yourself
or believe that you're all alone in the world.
Open yourself up to the possibilities of
finding like-minded friends.*

→

*Explore your local newspaper, magazines, yellow
pages, church or synagogue bulletins, gyms,
or department stores for organized activities
suited for women of size. Be daring and attend
an event. Take a friend if you need a little extra
courage. Call the organizer and get the name of
someone to speak with beforehand, so you
have someone to greet when you get there.
Or go alone and say hello to the first person
you see at the door.*

→

Create something just right for you, like a support group, a walking club, a reading club, or a cooking class. Advertise in the local paper, on the Internet, or spread the news by word of mouth. It will be worth the effort.

→

Section Three

Bountiful Women on the Move

Up, Up, and Away

*I was invited to my college roommate's first
wedding, at forty . . . I wanted to be there. Yet I
picked fights with my husband, imagined flu
symptoms . . . all to evade the plane. I simply
did not want to struggle to get comfortable
in the seat.* —GEORGINE

A bountiful woman is a woman on the move—she isn't sitting at home watching television shows depicting how great
other people's lives may be. She is out among the players—
taking trips, meeting new people, and risking unfamiliar circumstances. My heartfelt desire is that you will invest your
energy, not in coming up with excuses, even if you call them
reasons, as to why you can't participate fully in life, but in
creatively solving whatever obstacles your size may pose.

One ominous challenge for bountiful women on the move
is confronting air travel. From beginning to end, flying is an
experience created with slender people in mind. Those who
design the planes obviously are envisioning a particular body
type, even though half of the population can't fit comfortably
in those tiny seats, have trouble buckling their seat belts and

need much more legroom than is available. For many travelers of any size, the talk these days is of the sardine-like experience on planes.

Even Dear Abby gets letters about plane travel traumas. Recently she had a letter from a concerned person worried about her friend of over three hundred pounds who could not fit into the seat on an airplane. Abby told the "concerned" person to have her friend call the airline and tell them the situation. EEK! Who would do that? We already know the airlines are not inclined to understand our plight.

Flying can be so difficult that many bountiful women avoid traveling, even when they would enjoy a trip or need to travel for work. Georgine, a thirty-eight-year-old mother of two children, ages nine and twelve, admitted she was, "Worried and anxious before my last trip. I was invited to my college roommate's first wedding, at forty years old. I wanted to be there. Yet I imagined every way I could avoid going. I picked fights with my husband, imagined flu symptoms, tried to get my boss to say I was needed at the office—all to evade the plane.

I simply did not want to struggle to get comfortable in the seat. Even though I know airlines have extensions for the seat belts, I did not want to ask for one because then I would be admitting that I did not fit in this world. But flying without a seat belt also frightened me. What if there was turbulence? Something disastrous could happen. I worked myself up into a fit of anxiety.

"I eventually took a deep breath and focused on what mattered to me. 'I am who I am,' I thought to myself. 'Yes I am fat. And I matter.' I walked into that airport prepared to do what I needed to do to make this work for me. First, when checking in, I asked if there was a row with an extra seat and was told no, but at least I had asked. No one died. I did not pass out. I had simply said the words.

"Then I went to the gate, got on the plane, and, as I was going to my seat, I asked the flight attendant, looking her in the eyes, if I could have a seat belt extender. She asked for my seat number, and off we went in separate directions. Later, she came and found me, quietly handed me the extender and I breathed deeply, content with my triumph." Georgine had gotten what she needed in a preplanned, low-profile manner.

Forty-nine-year-old Martha, a CEO of a booming company, took a more forceful approach. Always cost conscious, she flew coach class. As she boarded the plane, she too asked for the extender. The flight attendant said she would bring it after her demonstration. Martha grinned as she told me, "I told her, 'No, I want it now. I do not want to be embarrassed by having you bring it to me at my seat.' She looked at me for a moment, and then handed me an extender."

Another challenge for bountiful women in flight is the increased likelihood of water retention. If you've ever taken your shoes off at the beginning of a flight, only to find they're two sizes too small at landing, you know what I mean. Ginny, who gives her age as "middle," offered a helpful suggestion.

A college professor, Ginny often travels to Europe to teach and give workshops. She's discovered a way to make her entire European experience more enjoyable. As soon as she boards the airplane, Ginny puts on compression stockings— the lighter-weight types of these stockings are available at drugstores. Wearing them on the plane goes a long way to reduce swelling.

"I discovered this," she explained, "after being on a trip where I had been on my feet all day teaching." Ginny smiled, "And I'd gone out partying all night after that! My feet and ankles swelled so much that I could not wear the shoes I had brought with me." Now she wears those stockings on the plane to manage the possible swelling. Her travel is much more comfortable due to this one tip.

I picked up a couple more helpful hints from Janelle, a motivational speaker who criss-crosses the country regularly. She told me, "When I started speaking on a national level, two things kept making my travel difficult. First, I didn't give myself time to walk the distance between the check-in counter and the departure gate at a reasonable pace. When you're on the road, it's a temptation to schedule too tightly, but I got tired of huffing of puffing around the airport, then boarding the plane hot and sweaty.

Janelle chuckled as she admitted, "At first I was angry, as if the airport was deliberately constructed to make me walk excessively far. Once I got over that notion, I asked myself, 'Okay, Jan, how are you going to master this situation?' The answer was simple and well within my control. I always make sure I arrive with an extra thirty minutes to spare, so I can stroll rather than dash to the gate."

Once on the plane, a second obstacle to Janelle's enjoyment posed itself: "Coping with those blasted tray tables!" Janelle exclaimed. "Not only am I a bountiful woman, I'm a full-breasted bountiful woman. Add to that the likelihood that the person in front of me tilts back in their chair, and there's no possible way one of those plastic tray tables will ever lay flat in front of me.

"At first I tried to force the table down, and nearly lost a breast over that maneuver!" she laughed. "Then I thought, 'Why do I need to use this thing at all? I'm not required to eat from the tray table.' So when the food service began, I asked the person in front of me to sit forward, just for the meal, then I placed my briefcase on my lap to make my own table. I thoroughly enjoyed the meal." Quite creative.

Janelle reminded me, "The challenges of traveling are fairly repetitive and predictable." "Plan ahead" is a helpful slogan for bountiful women on the move. Some airports seem to be designed for athletes training for long-distance runs rather than for your average person walking a reasonable span. Often maps of airports are available from travel agents or airlines. Check ahead regarding the distance between the curb and the boarding gate, making sure you give yourself plenty of time to make your destination cool, calm, and collected. Why wear yourself out before the trip begins?

And keep in mind other parts of the trip that might be uncomfortable. Your size does not mandate that you be squeezed, squashed, and sweaty. Remember, you have the right to be comfortable traveling as much as anyone else. So be proactive, and have a great flight!

More Secrets for Bountiful Living

Practice your request in your mind so it comes
out easily.

→

Secure an aisle or window seat.

→

If possible, travel in business or first class, or at
less busy times when coach seating isn't so
crowded.

→

Use a pillow or your carry-on bag on your lap if
the tray table won't go flat.

→

Ask the person ahead of you to sit upright
during food service.

→

Give yourself plenty of time to arrive at the
departure gate. Take a leisurely stroll, not a
mad dash, to your plane.

→

Let's Talk about Tiny Seats

*I had to fight an old theme in my head
that said "You don't fit. You're not entitled
to this kind of car," but I was tired of
being such a "nice girl." —*LOIS

Airplanes aren't the only places where we're asked to sit in too-tiny seats, or stuff our legs into cramped spaces, or strap ourselves in with short safety belts. Let's talk about cars.

Terry, a fifty-six-year-old attorney, had tackled many adversaries in her work. She was known as a powerhouse at her firm, and no one really wanted to take her on once she set her mind to a course of action. Married with two grown children, she was on the move from morning until night. As she sped through her day, she never strapped on her seat belt for one simple reason—it did not fit. Terry told me with a glint of mischief in her eyes, "I knew that wearing a seat belt was the law, and in general, I obey the law! Plus with all the safety information about using a seat belt, I knew I should. But to be honest with you, it just wasn't comfortable, and when I was wearing a coat, which was all winter, there wasn't a chance I could get the belt around me. So I simply chose not to think about it."

As a member of a support group for larger women, Terry was willing to listen to other members' concern over the danger involved. Terry said, "I realized that by not using my seat belt, I was actually limiting my life choices, even putting my life in jeopardy. If I never got into an accident, there would be no consequence, but none of us plans to have an accident. I deserve the same level of safety as anyone else." As a lawyer, Terry knew that there are laws in some states that require car dealers to make certain that the seat belt fits the primary driver of the car, regardless of that driver's size.

She continued, "I realized that all I had to do was ask for alterations to be made, although asking was not the easiest task for me." Terry laughed, "If I were acting on behalf of one of my clients, I'd have no trouble going after the best treatment, but to ask for myself, well, that was much harder.

"So I took a deep breath and called the parts department of my car dealership, requesting the seat belt extender. They actually had them in stock! I didn't want to deal with anyone face to face because I was worried they might hassle me about my size, or even glance at me in a way that would not feel okay, so I asked them to mail it to me rather than having to go pick it up. They happily complied, and I simply installed it myself. Easy; really, amazingly easy.

"I took courage from that experience, and was a bit more assertive when I purchased my next car. During the test-drive, I mentioned to the salesperson that the seat belt was snug and asked if the dealer would adjust that for me. He complied without batting an eye, seeing the adjustment as part of the deal. The fact is, every dealership has such extenders or can easily order them. If they want your business, then they'll include extenders in the sales package." Expect reasonable treatment and go after what you need to make your driving experience safe.

By the way, seat belt extenders are universal and fit on airline seat belts, too. Many stores that sell travel gear or automotive parts have them in stock. In some states, the automobile association has a catalog from which you can order them. All this information is simply a phone call away. Consider carrying an extender in your suitcase or briefcase, so whether you're traveling by plane, in someone else's car, or in a rental car, you can have the same peace of mind and level of ease as you have moving around your local area.

Terry made another helpful discovery. She told me, "I heard about a clip that parents use to hold straps in place for their children. This clip worked great for me, pulling the seat belt away from cutting into my neck. I didn't realize how much I dreaded driving until I took care of these two issues. Now getting around is a breeze."

Purchasing a new car can bring other issues to the forefront. Lois, thirty-one, is an emergency room social worker who needs a reliable car because she often works unusual hours. Her car was on its last leg, so she started thinking about getting a new one. She liked sports cars, being kind of racy herself, especially for being a social worker. She confessed, "I really wanted a red car, maybe even a convertible, with a leather interior. But I told myself, 'I'm a poor social worker—I should buy something reasonable.'"

Being enterprising, though, Lois went looking for what she actually wanted—a red sports car convertible that was also large enough for her to fit in comfortably. First, Lois searched on the Internet, looking at the websites for *Consumer Reports* and car magazines, to discover what her options were. Then she got on the telephone with dealers and asked questions about such items as interior room, specifying that she was a large and tall woman. Naturally, many dealers told her that they were sure she would fit, and to come on in. Lois pressed for the interior dimensions. She was loathe to spend days or weeks with dealers, so Lois stayed on the phone until she got the answers she was seeking. When all was said and done, she went to see three different cars.

Lois beamed, "I loved two of them, which were more than comfortable for my size. Next, I found a broker to search for the best price. I had to fight an old theme in my head that said, 'You don't fit. You're not entitled to this kind of car,' but I was tired of being such a 'nice girl.' I've been such a pleaser that I normally wouldn't have bothered the dealers with all of my questions. I'd have gotten some car that I didn't really want, and would have felt discouraged and depressed. This time, I responded to that message by saying to myself, 'I want what I want. I work hard. My dollar is as good as anyone else's.'"

Guess what? She got exactly what she wanted. In fact, after we spoke, she invited me to come outside and admire her new car. It was gorgeous! As Lois drove off waving in her red sports car with the top down, a leopard scarf tying back her hair and earrings dangling from her ears, she was not at all the image of the social worker you might expect. I could tell she felt stupendous about her car—and herself.

Cars aren't the only culprits in the small-seat challenge. Another hindrance to bountiful living is the theater seat, especially in older theaters. Philosophy student Robin loves the theater—opera, ballet, concerts, community plays, foreign films. But attending such events was nearly impossible without a great deal of courage and forethought. She lamented, "I spend most of my time attending class, reading books, talking to other scholars. At times, I just need a break, but I didn't feel comfortable going out, not even to the movies, because I often did not fit in the seats.

"My therapist asked me why I didn't bring my own chair or ask for one to be set up in the aisle. I told her that if I did that, everyone would know I am fat. As the words came out of my mouth, I realized how absurd they actually sounded. Anyone who sees me knows that I'm large. So why did I think showing up with a chair would let the cat out of the bag?"

Robin smiled, "The shame and denial were limiting my possibilities for enjoyment." Armed with this awareness, Robin put a folding chair in her car. She saw that *Around the World in Eighty Days,* a movie she had loved as a child, was showing at a nearby theater that played vintage movies. She went into the theater, found the seats too small, told the ticket taker she would be right back, and got the chair and her popcorn. She had a thrilling beginning to a new way of living, and she was proud of herself too.

With a little creativity, bountiful women can enjoy a full array of life-enhancing experiences. We can bring a suitable chair with us, maybe even keeping one in the car for spontaneous moviegoing; we can check with the theater ahead of time to make sure there's a chair available; we can go in early and try out the seats; we can purchase standing-room only tickets for the more costly performances; and, if we can afford it, we can splurge on box seats. The first step is deciding that we're worth the effort, and that we deserve to enjoy good entertainment just as much as anyone else does.

By and large, places designed for entertainment are built to accommodate thinner people. This is especially true for the various attractions and rides at amusement parks. Carolyn, now in her thirties, told me about an experience she had while on a date at an amusement park in her early twenties. She recalled, "We had a great time exploring the park, riding every single ride. We saved the roller coaster for the last ride of the day, imagining how exhilarating it would be.

"We waited in line forever, listening to the screams, squeals, and yells from those currently on the ride. Finally we were at the front of the line, ready to get on to the bench seats—two people in front and two in back. We sat down in the front and I tried to pull down the bar that would lock us into the car. I pulled and pulled, horribly embarrassed. I felt humiliated in front of my friend and the strangers who were sitting in the seat behind us. I had been looking forward to this ride all day, and I was determined to keep my seat, but I certainly didn't want to risk my or my date's life, so I kept pulling. I took in a deep, deep breath and the bar locked into place. Through the whole ride I was terrified that the bar would spring open and fling us both out of the car, but it held strong. I don't know if that added or detracted to our enjoyment of the ride. I think we were both giddy with the thrill of it all!"

Youthful exuberance aside, bountiful women deserve to enjoy amusement parks in safety, sit in theaters in comfort, and drive around town in style. Insist on taking your rightful place—behind the wheel or on a ferris wheel. I like how Carolyn put it: "I live in this world, and I make it work for me."

More Secrets for Bountiful Living

Go after what you need, now.

*Don't allow yourself to be physically unsafe,
in any circumstance—on a plane, in a car,
at an amusement park.*

*Feel your strength, your personal worth, as you
ask for what you need to make an experience
just right for you.*

Stretch yourself, do the hard thing, reach.

*Say to yourself, "I want what I want. I work
hard. This is business. My dollar is as good as
anyone else's."*

Enjoying Exercise?

Whenever I walk into the company gym . . . I say to myself, "You are allowed to go in here. What are they going to know about you that they don't already know by looking at you with your clothes on?" —ANDREA

The word "exercise" can trigger intense reactions from bountiful women, often because of the way many of us have punished ourselves physically trying to lose weight. It's not unusual to hear comments like, "I hate to exercise, I always have"; or "I have a horror of any kind of sport. It reminds me of embarrassing experiences in high school gym class"; or "I can't imagine going to an exercise class. How would I look in a leotard?"

Andrea, who at thirty-three works for a multinational corporation with a full gymnasium facility, recounted a miserable experience in high school regarding exercise. "At the time I was in school, the presidential fitness tests were required. Everyone had to run or walk a certain distance. At the end of the test, the teacher read every student's time out loud. When she read my time, everyone laughed." Andrea can still hear the laughter whenever she walks into the company gym, and she has had to work hard to overcome those memories. She says to herself, "You are allowed to go in here. What are they going to know about you that they don't already know by looking at you with your clothes on?"

In spite of painful associations with exercise, bountiful women are discovering that if they refer to it as "movement" or "moving for health," their strong feelings can fade into the background, allowing for a more full experience of their own bodies. Dana, forty-five and married with two sons, laughingly and lovingly spoke of the enlightening moment when she rejected the notion of exercising in order to lose weight and began to move for the pure enjoyment of it.

Recalling the last time she dieted, she told me, "I enrolled in one of the well-established weight-loss programs and gave it my all. I thought it was a great program, by far the most complete I had seen. And I lost weight."

Then she hit that all too familiar plateau, a place many people reach and a limited number are able to push past. The tide turned and her weight increased. Fearing that she was losing ground, she decided to find a therapist, someone who could help her continue to lose weight. Dana was surprised by what the psychologist told her. "I was expecting the usual weight-loss song and dance," Dana admitted. "Instead, the therapist said that she was not a weight-loss counselor, and that she believed people should focus on day-to-day decisions in taking the best care of themselves and should let their body in its wisdom figure out what size to be. 'That's your "healthy weight"—the weight your body is when you are living your life in a healthy way.' I'd never heard that before. Never. I have learned now to accept what I weigh at any moment as the weight my body needs to be. Now that I've accepted this, my life is working well. I exercise because I enjoy it. I am healthy, fit, active, and feel great about my life and future."

For Dana, as for many bountiful women, the concept of discontinuing the effort to change your body is completely novel. But try it. Rather than trying to change yourself, look at who you are and what you want in your life. Take good care of yourself by eating healthy foods and moving for sheer enjoyment. The goal is to have a full life, a good time, and fun, and not to achieve a specific number on the scale.

Once a woman's attitude shifts from "having to exercise" to "getting to move," a new level of happiness often results. Alice, a forty-eight-year-old publisher, had loved swimming as far back as she could remember, probably from the time she was seven or eight years old. Growing up, the center of her family life was the pool. She loved being in the water, even near the water.

"As I got older and lived on my own," she explained, "I gained weight and felt self-conscious wearing swimsuits and going to the public pool, so I stopped. Eventually my body became stiff and achy because I never moved it. I was so uncomfortable that I finally gave in and called all the pools in my area for rates and times. I also asked if there were any other larger women who went there to swim." While she was told that there were no particularly large people who went there to swim, several people she talked with encouraged her to come and try out their facility anyway.

Alice grinned, "Now I go almost every day in the late afternoon or evening. I have had incredible moments in the water. I feel sensual, I feel relaxed, I feel embodied—a totally pleasurable experience. It gives me time to think and meditate, see the colors in the sky, the blues, the pinks, and on other occasions, watch the stars." She added, "Swimming isn't a luxury. I have to do it. I need to do it. Without it, my emotional and spiritual energy is turned down, is closed in. When I am swimming, I feel open, alive, awake, aware."

On the question about showing her body in a bathing suit, she said, "No body is better than any other body. A body is a body. If someone looks, they look. When I feel the air on my body, I feel totally fine. It is my right to be in my body and enjoy it. Now I have about twenty bathing suits in all different colors and styles. I wear whatever enhances my mood."

Bodies were made for movement, and when we deprive ourselves of this essential nurturing, we suffer physically, emotionally, and spiritually. Sometimes it takes an illness to remind us that our bodies love to move. Anna, a forty-nine-year-old image consultant, faced her biggest challenge when she was diagnosed with diabetes. She had a family history of the disease and knew that there was a good possibility she would get it, regardless of her weight.

"Life changed from that moment forward," Anna told me. "I learned to eat many small meals instead of two or three large ones, and I had to watch my blood sugar frequently. The hardest part for me was my doctor's mandate to exercise. I've always hated to exercise, and my life is full without having to make room for something I despise." But despising exercise didn't change the fact that she had to find a way that worked for her. She thought about joining a gym, hiring a personal trainer, finding an exercise partner—she made a long list.

"Then I figured out what would work for me!" Anna exclaimed. "I knew I was easily bored so, instead of finding one exercise approach, I did them all!" On Mondays, she walked with her friend Kim. On Wednesdays, she had a personal trainer so that she would get a full workout. And on Saturdays, she went to a water aerobics class at a gym for women of substance. For her, having all the elements was the only way she felt assured that she would actually exercise. Her life depends on it, and a great life it is.

Exercise can be transformed into a social gathering, one of camaraderie and play. Claudia, a thirty-two-year-old legal assistant told me, "Ginny, Lorna, MaryAnn, and I met in a water aerobics class. Early mornings we put on bathing suits, something which many of us have not done in years, and toddle off to class. We ski, hop, jog, punch, stretch, and do what they call 'shoot throughs' in the water for forty-five minutes each day. I actually have a great time and feel quite self-righteous that I am doing this good thing for myself. We compare notes on where to find bathing suits since they disintegrate after day-to-day use in the chlorinated water, the latest way to strengthen our bodies, and groan when our instructor tells us to just do four more of the latest move. If you groan, it makes those moves easier to do!"

Groaning can be fun. Just ask Jennifer, a fifty-four-year-old hairdresser who not only works out at her gym every day, she's become quite the weight lifter. Jennifer has struggled with arthritis and joint problems due to her family history and her weight. Her symptoms have caused her substantial emotional and physical stress. When she found a gym where she could be comfortable and work out as frequently as she wished, she immediately began to feel better.

"I huff and puff as I lift those weights," Jennifer acknowledges, "but I've never felt better in my life. It was worth facing the embarrassment I initially felt about how different my body looked than most of the others' who come here. But I found a place where I could be healthy, exercise vigorously, and be myself."

Maybe lifting weights, water aerobics, or other more organized exercise is not the ticket for you. One size does not fit all, as we bountiful women know. You might be more comfortable following in the footsteps of sixty-year-old Grace, a large, wise woman and spiritual presence. Her heart overflows with ways to make a difference in her community, but her health was suffering from late nights doing what others needed. She was exhausted, but always had more to do, more to give.

Finally, her physician prevailed and told her that she had to slow down or she would not live to provide what meant so much to others. While she had ignored his warnings on many other occasions, this time she heard something in his voice that got her attention. She was scared and worried, but mostly she wanted to be sure that she had time to watch and participate in the lives of the children she adored. She knew that she had to do something to start moving her body. But she also knew that going to a gym or being with other people wouldn't work for her.

Being a spiritual person, her choice was to have more time in nature. Grace told me, "I gave myself permission to walk through a grove of trees in a park near my home. Five minutes among the trees was what I thought I could spare. While I knew it was not much, those five-minute daily interludes saved my life." Every single day for three months, she walked into the grove of trees, looked up at the light, felt the air, took some deep breaths, and thought to herself, this is what the doctor ordered. Every single day for three months, she came home and went back to her community service projects.

"Then one day while in the grove of trees," she said, her eyes lighting up, "I got curious about some wildflowers just beginning to grow. I observed their color and shape. That day, I was in the grove for almost fifteen minutes. On my way home, I stopped at the library to learn the names of the flowers so I could tell the children I would see that afternoon. By the time I came home, an hour had passed. I realized then that I did have time to move, and that it wasn't just a waste of time or a luxury." Almost every day from then on, Grace spent some substantial time in nature, observing, breathing, relaxing, and being, all in the name of spiritual, emotional, and physical health, all from a five-minute beginning.

Your body loves to move. Why allow negative experiences from the past to rob you of this joyous opportunity? Discard the label of "exercise" and replace it with whatever works for you—dancing, strolling, exploring, floating, or stretching, for example. Your body will thank you for taking back your power and reclaiming the right and possibility of healthy movement.

More Secrets for Bountiful Living

Begin where you are, with five minutes if
that's all you have, and move. Bring oxygen into
your lungs, then push it down into your stomach
as you allow your limbs to stretch and
the blood to flow.

→

Small doses of fitness can make a difference. Do
modest bits—they add up.

→

Finding a buddy makes it easier for some and
harder for others. Do what you need.

→

Would dancing do it for you? Maybe gardening
is your passion, or a stroll around the mall.
Enjoyment, pleasure, flexibility, balance,
endurance, and strength are the goals.

→

Say to yourself, as Alice does,
"No body is better than any other body.
A body is a body. If someone looks, they look."

→

Consider that your "good weight" is "whatever
weight" your body is when you are living your
life in a healthy way, eating reasonably, moving,
resting, and having fun.

→

Surviving a Trip to the Doctor

Discouraged, I left and told Suzanne about the visit. Suzanne was infuriated and outraged on my behalf and insisted that I go back immediately and say, "If I was a thin person now, what would you do next?" —RACHEL

Rachel didn't feel well. She also didn't feel like going to see the doctor, knowing she'd most likely get little assistance and a big lecture on losing weight. She knew all about doctors and what they said to patients, because Rachel was a physician herself. At forty-two, she was involved in genetic research at a prestigious teaching hospital, and was well-versed in attitudes about weight and dieting.

She told me, "I had felt poorly for so many weeks, perhaps months at that point, that I couldn't recall feeling okay. It was easier for me to tolerate poor health, though, than face a fellow doctor. Fortunately, my friend Suzanne kept urging me to go for a checkup. I didn't listen to her at first, but eventually she nagged me enough that I agreed and made an appointment. Just as I expected, the doctor decided nothing was wrong with me and told me to lose weight. If I still didn't feel well after I was thinner, I should return. Discouraged, I left and told Suzanne about the visit. Suzanne was infuriated and outraged on my behalf and insisted that I go back immediately and say, "If I was a thin person now, what would you do next?"

"To his credit, the physician heard me, did some tests, and found a growth in my colon. I had surgery and they found that the tumor was malignant. I've been receiving chemotherapy and radiation, and now have a chance at life, an opportunity that would have been lost for me if I'd waited until I lost weight to be treated with the same respect thin people receive. Those words, 'If I was a thin person now,' may have saved my life."

Rachel's story struck a chord for me personally. My father was a physician, and I was all too familiar with the negative biases held in the medical community. I used to say to doctors, "If I was your wife or daughter, how would you treat me?" I tried to get doctors to see me as a person who was entitled to adequate medical services.

Quality medical care became a critical issue for me in 1999, when I was on my way to have lunch with some friends and had almost reached the door of the restaurant. The heel of my flat shoe caught the edge of a hole in the sidewalk. I fell, slamming my head on a concrete planter. My friends got a tablecloth from the restaurant to cover me and called the paramedics.

I was terrified knowing that I'd suffered a serious head

trauma, one that might leave me permanently impaired. I immediately went to see my doctor and then a neurologist. In this age of managed care, when every service is scrutinized for the risk/benefit ratio (and some doctors benefit financially by not providing care), the neurologist was hesitant to authorize tests to determine whether any damage had been done in the fall. I asked for a Magnetic Resonance Imaging (MRI) scan to rule out devastating possibilities—such scans of the head can cost close to $2,000. The doctor looked at me and said nothing. I asked again. He still said nothing and started writing in his notes. I kept talking, thinking that he would have to respond at some point. "Not only do I want an MRI, I want the scan done in an open machine because I know I will be more comfortable, less afraid. I won't be comfortable until I get a definitive answer."

Tears of vulnerability and terror were building. I was persistent. I was respectful. And still, he said nothing. He looked away. I wondered if he had died, he was so still. It seemed as if hours had passed. I thought afterward that it was like a horror movie where you are sitting across from someone who could save you from impending danger or a threatening event and he just sits there not saying or doing anything.

He finally acquiesced and reluctantly arranged for the scan. As I left the office feeling totally disoriented by my fall and his unconscionable and unethical behavior, I believe I heard him say to his nurse, "Should I order an MRI for every overweight, middle-aged woman who falls?" If he had had the nerve to say that directly to me, I would have said a definitive, "Yes."

Fortunately, the results of the MRI showed that nothing was amiss. Once I got the results of the test, I never went back to that doctor. His callous bias lost him a patient, and naturally I passed on the information about how he had treated me to other professional people in my community.

When any of us go to the doctor, we are looking to someone with expertise who can help us. We are in a vulnerable situation and need to know that someone is there to take care of us, to help us, to give us the information that we do not have. The doctor-patient relationship is a partnership or it is nothing at all.

Unfortunately many doctors have biases against larger people. Directly confronting the size/weight bias that some physicians exhibit can diminish its power. Many physicians will take a step back and rethink their diagnosis and treatment plan when we help them find a way to think of us, not as "fat women," but as human beings who deserve quality medical care like everyone else. If a doctor becomes defensive or focuses solely on weight, then it's time to find someone else who can see past the pounds. It is possible, believe me. Call a new physician's office directly and ask about his or her attitude in regards to treating a large person.

It might be difficult to go to the doctor when you feel poorly, if you suspect you might have a serious illness or injury, or when you know you need routine medical checkups. The next time you find yourself procrastinating, ponder Rachel's experience or my experience. Rachel said, "If I hadn't gone to the doctor when I did, gotten an accurate diagnosis and helpful treatment, I most likely wouldn't be here today." While you will most certainly survive a trip to the physician, you might not survive without one.

Dana, an aerobics instructor, acknowledged that being a physician's daughter may have given her an edge, at the outset, to feeling entitled to ask doctors for what she needed. She was not intimidated by physicians, knowing that they are people like everyone else, not gods. Typically she would get a referral from a person or place that she respected, having requested a physician who was able to treat people of whatever size.

Remember what you expect, what you feel entitled to, from your physician goes a long way in getting what you want and need. People often think that doctors know all, see all, be all, are all. Many people turn over much or all of their power to their doctors when they go to them. Doctors are human, too, and they simply have a body of knowledge, a different body of knowledge than you have as a patient, about what is happening with you. If the help is going to be meaningful to you, it has to be a true partnership. You must feel entitled to ask for that and to object when it's not given. One thing that is helpful is to be armed with information.

Information, and a little outrage, can go a long way in a doctor's office. Just ask Martha who was infuriated when she went to her gynecologist's office for her annual exam and was asked to put on a paper gown "that didn't even cover one of my breasts!" Martha fumed. "I turned to the nurse and demanded to see the person in charge. When the manager arrived, I said, 'I know I'm not the only woman of my size who comes to this office. I've seen them in the waiting room. We are your customers. To protect our modesty, you need to provide us with gowns that fit!'" The next time Martha went to the doctor, the office manager had ordered different styles of gowns to see which would work best for their patients. She thanked Martha. Martha's confrontation paid off. As it turned out, this particular office, like many others, was willing to be reminded by its patients of what they needed. They were receptive and responsive to Martha's requirements, as they should be.

Another bountiful woman stood up for herself by refusing to step one foot on that ghastly scale. When asked to step on the scale, Lisa, a thirty-eight-year-old scientist, simply responded, "'I don't do scales.' The nurse said, 'What do you mean you don't do scales?' I said, 'I don't do scales.' We squared off for a moment, looking each other in the eyes, and then she said, 'Okay. You don't do scales!'"

Like Lisa, Ginny hates to be weighed, but takes a different approach. She told me, "I believe that it's helpful to the doctor to know my weight, I just don't want to know it! I get on the scale with my back to the numbers and ask the nurse not to tell me how much I weigh. The doctor gets the information needed, and I don't leave the office depressed, with that haunting number echoing in my head."

Let Andrea, thirty-three, be another example to us. She went to see a doctor because she was fatigued all the time. The doctor told her to join a weight-loss program and she would feel better. Andrea responded, "I have been the same weight for the last ten years, and I have only been fatigued for the past two months. The two conditions are not linked." The doctor again recommended weight loss. Andrea continued, "Are you telling me that if I won't join a program, you won't give me the help I'm seeking?" That was exactly what the doctor was telling her, so Andrea left and found someone else who was more responsive to her symptoms.

As these women have demonstrated, it's critical that you make your preferences known so your physician and nurses can properly care for your medical needs. Don't allow yourself to be dismissed because of your size, or to have your symptoms routinely diagnosed as weight related. How well you advocate for yourself is not merely important, it could be the difference between life and death.

More Secrets for Bountiful Living

Be informed. The National Association to Advance Fat Acceptance puts out pamphlets on the rights of larger people to have positive relationships with their bodies and weight, and on what is adequate medical care.

→

Have concrete information that you can discuss with your physician to see whether you can create a real partnership that could make a huge difference in your care. This is a way to help them help you.

→

Speak up. If your physician is not prepared for someone of your size, simply ask for what you need. If they won't provide it, save your energy and go elsewhere. You are the customer.

→

Plan ahead. Get recommendations from other bountiful women. Call and talk to the physician or staff ahead of time, and ask whether they can accommodate your particular needs. If yes, go in. If not, don't put yourself in a difficult situation. Don't be shamed because of your size.

→

Remember: You require and deserve good medical care. Period.

→

All in a Day's Work

As we bountiful women know from personal experience, negative attitudes about larger people abound in the workplace. A successful bountiful woman is one who finds effective solutions to coping with this unfair bias.

Bountiful women often have to prove themselves to be capable far beyond their thinner colleagues, male or female. We can be angry about it, sulk about it, gripe about it, organize and become political about it—all those possibilities are okay. But after that, we still have to combat it to achieve our goals. Bountiful women are up to the challenge, and, in spite of the obstacles, are insisting on their rightful place in the workforce.

Take Kelly for example, a twenty-seven-year-old business owner and housepainter. She was tomboy as a kid, wanting to make her own money to buy tapes of the music she loved. She went to work with the man next door, who owned his own house-painting business. Kelly was a terrific housepainter. She was exacting, patient, neat, and worked extremely hard. Best of all, she had an eye for color and a knack for making combinations work. When Kelly went off to community college, her neighbor told her parents that she would always have a job with him.

However, while at college she began to gain weight. When she approached her neighbor for a job a year or two later, he hesitated. She persisted. Finally he admitted that he felt she had gotten too fat—that working on ladders would be unsafe, and that she would not be able to carry all the paint, tarps, and so on, that were part of the job. Kelly declared, "I was very resentful, insulted, and hurt, but I knew I could still do the job, so I kept after him. I told him, 'Give me a chance. If it doesn't work out, you don't have to pay me.' He figured he had nothing to lose, so he agreed."

Not only did Kelly do a great job, but when her neighbor decided to retire, he asked Kelly if she wanted to take over his business! She smiled, "I have more painting business now than I can handle. It's great being an entrepreneur with people working for me. There are a few things I don't do, but then that's true about everyone who works for me. I've got one employee with bursitis in his shoulder, so he can only do certain jobs. Another guy has knee problems, so climbing ladders is out for him. We all have our limitations and our gifts." Kelly is making a success of her business because she started from the ground up, and knows the business inside and out. She still works as a colorist, and sometimes returns as a painter when the job requires her careful touch. Once given the chance, Kelly proved herself more than capable of doing the job.

But sometimes we let our attitudes get in the way of moving forward in our careers. Thirty-year-old Janine, who recently received a Ph.D. in sociology, was applying for a teaching job at a research institute. After several positive interviews, Janine was turned down for the job. She could not understand why. Janine told me, "It just didn't make sense to me. My qualifications were exactly what they were looking for. I was so disappointed that I decided to find out what had happened. When I inquired, I received the standard response that they had found someone who fit their needs more completely. But I didn't believe it. Something was not being said.

"I called Joan, a woman with whom I had developed a rapport during the interviewing process. Joan said that, of course, she could not tell me anything officially, but she thought the issue was my appearance, meaning my size. I was stunned, embarrassed, and offended. I have worked hard to obtain an excellent education and superior references, yet I was not hired because I am large. I tried to rationalize what Joan said, hoping that she was mistaken, or maybe vindictive, but somehow it rang true. I decided to contact the chairman of the department. To his credit, he agreed to meet with me. I practiced my questions, wanting to be respectful, and went to talk with him.

"I told him how disappointed I was about not being hired for the position, and asked him to be honest with me, while acknowledging that I knew he couldn't, or at least shouldn't, admit to discrimination. I looked him in the eye, person to person, and asked for his counsel and direction.

"He was straight with me, saying that all of my qualifications were in place. He said, 'However, the institute sells our services to some of the most successful businesses in this area. We are judged by the people we send there. Our employees have learned to present themselves as much like the customer as possible. We typically send a person or a team out to determine the dress code of the people with whom we will be interacting before we even go for our first meeting with them. Not matching what our clients expect of their employees makes it much less likely that we will get the contract.'"

Janine realized at that moment that her own attitudes about her size were interfering with her desire for advancement. While her clothing was clean and pressed, she loathed shopping and had not updated her wardrobe for several years. She had not been conscientious about style and appropriate dress, hoping her education and references were sufficient.

Being the person she was, Janine simply asked whether he would be willing to interview her again in a week. He said yes. Janine arrived the next week in well-fitting, professional attire, and she was hired for the next available opening. Through this episode, she learned to think critically and to problem solve in a creative way. Even though she was large, when she met the institute's need for a certain professional appearance, she got the job. She could have assumed that she was not hired because of her weight. Instead she decided to go after the information that would help her determine what actually had happened.

Obviously, it is not always possible to get the inside scoop. And there are frequently additional hoops for a large woman to jump through in finding her place in the businessworld. Some hoops you'll be willing to jump through. Some, not.

As we bountiful women know from personal experience, negative attitudes about larger people abound in the workplace. A successful bountiful woman is one who finds effective solutions to coping with this unfair bias. Sometimes the best solution is to confront the prejudice head-on, as did Nancy, a thirty-five-year-old physical therapist. She is respected and has been treated well in almost every work situation. But then there was Joe, another therapist, who made many insulting remarks.

She said, "I frequently have flowers on my desk and he would say, 'Did you buy yourself flowers again?' or, 'Oh, do you really want to be eating *that*?' At first I stewed about his comments, but then I decided to put my foot down. I approached him and said, "I need to talk to you. You don't have to like me, but I never want you to make another comment like that to me again.' He responded by saying that he was clearly kidding. I said, 'Never say one of those things again.' He stopped. However, a few days later, Joe slipped back into his old behavior. I looked at him in a neutral way, not angrily, not friendly—just looked at him. He got it. He said, 'No offense?' I smiled, and never again did I have to erect such a strong firewall to protect myself."

Insensitive remarks from coworkers abound, as do the many ways we can respond to them. One of the most direct responses I've heard about came from Lisa, a thirty-eight-year-old manager at a biotechnology company, who overheard colleagues talking about how every overweight person is lazy and should lose weight. She said, "I was stunned that these educated people would speak in this manner. I walked around the corner and when they saw me, silence fell over the group. I couldn't go up and slap them silly, even though that's what I felt like doing. Instead I said, 'Even if I sound like an angry fat woman, I've got to tell you that you don't know what you're talking about. You're spouting the same worn-out dogma that hasn't worked for millions of people. Can't you come up with something new?' I could tell these people were thinking, 'Oh my God, she actually said that!'" Lisa smiled, "Hasn't been a lot of discussion about other people's so-called weight problems around the office lately!"

Another bountiful woman was confronted with negative comments, not from a coworker, but from a client. Lany, forty-two, had worked extremely hard to find her place in the world after tackling her alcohol addiction. She went to meetings, talked to her sponsor, did her step work, and was committed to finding her own answers. As time passed in her recovery, she took on the professional role of an alcohol abuse counselor. One of her duties was to give presentations for clients who were struggling with their own addiction to alcohol. Comfortable in her skin, Lany was caught off guard when a woman spoke up during a presentation and accused her of being addicted to food, just as she had been to alcohol. Lany realized that it was easy for someone who was thin to assume that all larger people were addicted to food. She told me, "I know what it's like to be addicted to a substance, and addiction is not the source of my larger size. There is not one simplistic cause. But I knew that if I engaged in explaining myself, I'd come off as defensive, and the woman would not only have the upper hand, I would undermine my effectiveness in helping her in the future.

"So I paused. The room was painfully silent. Instead of allowing the focus to be placed on my issues, I turned my attention to helping the client. She was new to the program, so I didn't know what had triggered such a hostile remark. I simply mirrored back what she had said, asking for clarification. In a gentle way, I held her accountable for her comment, and she backpedaled immediately. I was careful not to embarrass her or return her hostility. After the meeting, she came up to me and apologized for her comment. Subsequently, she's been quite successful in our program and has now been sober for three and a half months."

Some find the direct approach works best for them, while others quietly make their way, demonstrating that size does not interfere with job performance. Being healthy and active are necessary for some positions, as is true for Cecelia, a forty-year-old high school vice principal. When asked about the demands of her job, she told me, "I'm frequently moving around talking to teachers, students, and parents. The campus of my school is spread out, and I imagine I walk several miles a day. That wouldn't be so bad if I could wear running shoes, but I'm in professional garb so I don't get that luxury."

To minimize wear and tear on her feet and legs, Cecelia purchased the most comfortable and best-fitting shoes possible. She groaned, "That's a start, but there is no appropriate footwear for the kind of walking I do every day. But I dare not complain. My profession is very competitive, and any admission that I might not be capable of the job could cost me my position. So I have a secret plan," Cecelia smiled. "I can come up with the best reasons for sitting down for a few minutes! I know exactly where all the chairs and benches are located around campus, so I use those rest stops as opportunities to chat with students or make a spontaneous connection with a teacher. If my feet hurt, I take care of them, just as I do everything else."

Competency and ingenuity are two words that capture the spirit of a bountiful woman. And, perhaps, maintaining a good sense of humor about it all! The epitome of these characteristics is Lorna, a fifty-five-year-old hairdresser, who is on her feet most of the day. Enterprising and innovative, Lorna explained, "Standing up and leaning over people fixing hair causes my lower back to tighten, plus my feet swell and my legs ache." She grinned, "Not a pretty picture. Growing up, my brother was in a wheelchair, so I was used to the idea of someone sitting to do what they need to do and still getting things done. I took my inspiration from him." Lorna bought an office chair with wheels that can be adjusted to any height she needs for different activities at the salon. "This makes a huge difference in the wear and tear on my body.

"When I get home at night, I still have housework. So I got another chair for my kitchen. I just roll around and around." Lorna also purchased a large cutting board for her kitchen table, so she's able to sit and do her food chopping, cutting, and preparation. Then she zooms around the kitchen and does all her other tasks sitting down. She only stands when she has to. And she very much enjoys spinning around while cooking.

"The whole arrangement saves energy for the things that I have to do on my feet," Lorna beams. "Not only are there chairs with rollers at work and in my kitchen, but I also have one outside by the washer and dryer. It's great for sitting and sorting laundry, folding clothes, and whatever else I need to do there. I wheel around to water plants, too. When I'm especially tired, I use one to vacuum or to scrub the tub. I have even used one like a walker when my back pain has hindered my ability to walk." This solution has allowed Lorna the freedom to do much more than would be possible without her resourcefulness. She has discovered, as many bountiful women have— that our so-called limitations can be opportunities for creative problem solving. While we cannot control other people's reactions to our size, we can make sure that we don't limit ourselves or unnecessarily reject exciting opportunities.

Some of the bountiful women I've spoken with work in settings that fully accept their size. The obstacle to advancement? Their own biases against themselves. Louise, at forty-five, almost kept herself from the opportunity to work on an international level. An accomplished presenter and computer expert, Louise taught large groups of between one hundred and two hundred hardware and software engineers. She was so effective that she was offered the opportunity to give her seminar to the upper management of her company—which meant that she would travel to Boston, London, and other fabulous places as yet undetermined. Louise froze at the suggestion.

With wide eyes, she explained, "I was so complimented and affirmed by the opportunity, but I was afraid of how difficult it would be to travel. Also, the company placed a lot of importance on physical fitness. Even though it was a telecommunications firm, there was a gymnasium on every campus of the company, and events centered around fitness and an attitude about size that made me uncomfortable. I didn't know whether I'd encounter more disapproval the higher up I went in the company."

Initially, she attempted to delay the travel decision for six months, imagining that that would give her time to lose weight and become thin and ready for the road. Rolling her eyes at those thoughts, Louise said, "Right. What was I thinking? I soon realized that I needed to go for this new adventure or let it pass me by. It was up to me."

Louise spoke to her therapist, her family, her friends. Everyone told her that this was a chance not to be missed. So, drawing on her support network, she went for it. She said, "I consulted with a friend of mine who is also large and who really knows how to dress for success. The clothing I typically wore to work didn't matter much since I usually made my presentations to grungy, supremely casual engineers. But that wouldn't work for the top echelon. Shopping for better clothes was worth the effort once I got in front of my first crowd; I realized that people in management had a uniform of sorts. Instead of rebelling against the corporate climate, I embraced it and put together a wardrobe that was appropriate, yet expressed my personal style. My evaluations have been glowing! I'm so glad I didn't hold myself back out of tremendous fear."

Louise gathered her strength and called for the help she needed. She was willing to stretch beyond what she had previously seen as her limit, finding that her stubbornness that had served her so well in her career could have a downside. She had to discover her accommodating, flexible side as well, and learned when to stand her ground and when to cooperate.

Bountiful women can be the most talented, resourceful, intelligent, and committed people in the workforce. There is no reason to hold yourself back or to tolerate being in corporate systems that are discriminating and critical. Find work environments that are encouraging and motivating. If you lean that way, become politically active to change the laws.

More Secrets for Bountiful Living

Save your energy for doing the essential
things that will keep your life moving ahead.
Raise the table, lower the chairs, raise the
kitchen counter, lower the towel bars, whatever
it takes to make life easier.

➔

Share your skills with those who appreciate
them and deserve them.

➔

Find and build alliances with coworkers who
know the score, creating power bases. Don't
isolate yourself because you feel different due to
your size. That will severely limit your success.

➔

Be analytical and intellectual when
you need to be.

➔

Become politically active, if that is your bent. Changing discriminatory laws regarding hiring just occurred in San Francisco; it can happen other places, too.

→

A job is a job no matter how good it is. It has to fit into your life, not be your life.

→

Eating Out on the Town

*It's too easy for us bountiful women
to deprive ourselves of relaxed,
enjoyable experiences.*

In a society that for the most part disapproves of larger people, eating in public can be anxiety- and shame-producing.
After all, we're *eating!* And that, some would contend, is our
biggest problem. Deborah, a forty-one-year-old retailer, was
acutely aware of what other people thought about her food
choices. Rather than order what she wanted to eat, Deborah
selected what she imagined other people thought she *should*
eat. Looking back on that time in her life, Deborah said, "I
don't know if people I ate with, or who sat near me in a
restaurant, actually believed that I should order a salad or
something low-calorie, since obviously I never asked them. I
just assumed that they would disapprove, and so I would
often select something I didn't really want.

"The worst part of this behavior was that immediately
upon arriving home after dining out, I'd raid the fridge and
binge out of a sense of deprivation and anger. I'd say to
myself, 'How dare they judge me?' to justify the fact that I'd

ordered something I didn't want to eat. What a way to live! When I realized what I was doing and how utterly ridiculous it was, I was floored that I was treating myself so miserably. And I thought other people were the oppressors whether they were or not. No more of that!"

Indeed. Whether Deborah was imagining disapproval or accurately reading the nonverbal cues of those around her, she has since decided that to live bountifully, she will order exactly what she wants to eat and enjoy every bite. She sighs with contentment, "Now I come home satisfied with my meal and say to myself, 'I am who I am, and if they cannot accept me, okay. That is just how it will be.'"

Not only does Deborah order what she wants, she politely insists that the food be cooked to order and the service be responsive. "I can't believe how much I used to limit myself because of the old voices in my head—voices that said things like, 'Don't send this back even though it's too raw; you're heavy and don't deserve to have this steak the way you like it,' or 'Don't make a scene about the fact that you never got your french fries; you really shouldn't have them anyway,' or "You don't want people to give you a negative look or make comments, do you?' Now if I don't like it, I send it back. I'm polite, but firm, just what I'd expect any of my friends to do in the same situation."

In addition to ordering what she enjoys, Deborah realizes that she deserves to be comfortable while she dines. "Rather than stuff myself into a booth to please other people, I simply state, 'No booth, please.' No one who is really my friend minds sitting at a table. Also, I ask for an armless chair, so I don't have to contend with feeling crowded at the table. If I've never been to a particular restaurant before, I call ahead to make sure that they can accommodate my needs and wishes. I'm simply no longer willing to suffer through a meal." And why should she? Maybe it would be more convenient for others if Deborah never spoke up, but this is Deborah's life and it's up to her to advocate for what she needs to enjoy it. Other people may not even notice if she is uncomfortable, but her life is not a dress rehearsal for something better yet to come.

Since the first person we encounter at a restaurant is the host, it may be helpful to make your preferences known initially, before you find yourself weaving and squeezing between tables and chairs and interrupting other people's meals. Martha commented, "As someone in the workforce, you'd think a host would learn by experience. One look and a competent host could make choices that would be pleasant for all concerned. The excellent hosts do, of course."

Martha smiled, "Actually, most will respond to my requests politely and efficiently. But if I encounter someone who doesn't quite get it, I simply get their attention and say, 'Look at me. Look at where you're leading us. Please make this easier.' I can be a bit confrontational at times, but I try to smile while standing up for myself. Usually the host will crack a smile and lead us in another direction." While you don't need to be afraid of seeming "difficult," you'll rarely need to be overpowering in your requests. Remember that you are competent and can handle whatever situations you encounter.

Eating out alone poses additional challenges for bountiful women. Most of us don't enjoy sitting by ourselves in restaurants, and this was certainly the case for Ashley, a single mother at forty-one and a nursing home administrator. She confessed, "Eating out alone was even less desirable the more weight I gained, but I often needed to eat out for lunch, or even for breakfast, depending on my work schedule.

"Sitting there by myself, I'd wonder whether people were making unfavorable judgments of me for being large and for being by myself. One time I thought to myself, 'Enough is enough!' Scanning the room, I saw lots of people chatting in an animated way. No one was concerned with me, so I decided to act as if everything was okay, even though I felt some anxiety. I opened a magazine and was soon absorbed in an article. What a wonderful feeling—to feel good about myself. And why not?"

Why not, indeed. It's too easy for us bountiful women to deprive ourselves of relaxed, enjoyable experiences. Bolster up your courage, grab a good book or crossword puzzle, or simply sit quietly to meditate, and enjoy the time you have to yourself as you savor a good meal—even a dessert! And speaking of dessert, let's talk about ice cream!

Alice loved ice cream. Now a sixty-three-year-old retired government worker, she recalled how her parents had used ice cream as the great reward for a job well done. The association between good things and ice cream stuck. She eats ice cream frequently at this point in her life.

"However," Alice recalled, "there was a time when I never ordered ice cream at a restaurant, or any other kind of dessert for that matter. And I'd certainly never walk down the street eating an ice cream cone! Partly I had learned that nice girls don't eat on the street, and partly I didn't want to confirm people's supposed assumption that I was fat because I ate bad stuff like ice cream all the time! How limiting of me. Even if someone did think that about me, why should I care? I should get to do what I want, when I want, especially at this point in my life."

On top of depriving herself of desserts, Alice had gotten into the habit of being "good" all day, which meant she ate next to nothing. At night, famished and feeling entitled to a reward, Alice would eat more than she actually enjoyed. A nutritionist told her that if she ate more of what she enjoyed during the day, she'd be less hungry at night and more motivated, physically and emotionally, to make choices that were more satisfying.

Alice continued, "With a new attitude, I went to a favorite restaurant whose motto is, 'This is a bad place to eat if you are on a diet.' I was no longer on one, so I ordered their hot fudge sundae on a chocolate brownie. Yum. I sat, slurped to myself, and enjoyed every single spoonful until I could eat no more. It was wonderful. I don't do this every day, only when I feel like it."

Let's face it. No one literally takes food away from us as we dine in a restaurant—we allow perceived attitudes against weight to influence what we order and how we enjoy our meal.

Cast aside whatever condemnation you suspect is lurking in the heads of others, and order what you want, what is healthy, what is right for you. Enjoy!

More Secrets for Bountiful Living

Do what you do and surrender the outcome.
Whatever judgments other people make are
about them, not you.

→

Savor every single morsel you select for yourself.
Mindful attention to what you are eating can
make it all the more delectable.

→

Eat what you choose—eating in a reactive way
still gives others power over you.

→

Eat a variety of foods, including fruits and
vegetables and whatever else makes for
healthy eating.

→

Say to yourself, "I have the choice to eat
what I want."

→

Assuming the Worst

I used to assume that if someone didn't invite me to a party . . . the reason was my weight. . . . Now that I'm more accepting of my own body, it occurs to me that there might be a variety of reasons why I don't click with someone else. —DONNA

While confronting discrimination is part of creating the safety we need, bountiful living also includes controlling our own tendencies to make negative assumptions. We don't like it when we're misunderstood. Becoming more understanding of others, and assuming good faith in confusing moments, can contribute to a deeper sense of self-acceptance as well as smoother relationships. We can be so transfixed on our size that it might be incomprehensible to us that others, quite frankly, don't care or don't notice.

Perhaps the most poignant story I heard was from Tanzy, who spoke about how her interpretation of other people's comments depends on her mind-set. "My mom has Alzheimers, and, sadly, she's at the 'I can't remember who you are' stage. She didn't recognize me, so I said, 'I'm your daughter, Tanzy.'

"She said, 'Wow, you've really gotten big!' My first thought was that she was commenting on my weight, but then I realized, 'Oh, she still thinks of me as her little girl. She's surprised that I've grown up.' My first response was rooted in my old way of thinking, all those negative judgments that cause me to be defensive, even when I don't need to be. It's easy to make assumptions about what people mean rather than being open to a variety of intentions."

While most of us don't want to be defensive, it can be a challenge coming up with positive, or even neutral, interpretations of comments people make. Pauline, an instructor at an alternative high school, described an encounter with a neighbor in which she tried to be as positive as possible. She said, "I was getting out of my car after a long day teaching. I'd been on my feet all day, and my neighbor pointed out that my feet seemed swollen in my high-heeled shoes. My first reaction was that she, being a petite woman, was being critical of me.

But the fact was, I didn't know for sure. Instead of defending myself by saying something like, 'Your feet would be swollen too if you had a day like mine,' implying, you critical person you! I consciously decided to take her comment as one of concern. She might have meant something else, but so what. I chose how I wanted to respond, and I said, 'Thanks for your concern. Yes, my feet do hurt.'" Pauline's neighbor went on to describe a long flight to Japan when her feet had swollen, and how uncomfortable it had been for her. Pauline's choice to assume good faith was well-founded;

rather than a negative judgment, her neighbor was offering comfort and empathy.

In a perfect world, perhaps everyone would like everyone else. But we all have preferences and favorites, pet peeves, and people who rub us the wrong way. Donna laughed about learning to cope with the fact that someone might not think she's as terrific as she thinks she is. "I used to assume that if someone didn't invite me to a party or didn't take me in as a close friend, the reason was my weight. I couldn't imagine there being any other reason. Now that I'm more accepting of my own body, it occurs to me that there might be a variety of reasons why I don't click with someone else. I have thin friends who don't get along with everyone they meet. Why should it be any different with me?"

Pat, an outgoing bountiful woman, discovered a similar truth as she became more loving toward herself. Always ready to welcome new people to her synagogue, Pat would occasionally greet a visitor who responded coolly. She explained, "At first I assumed they didn't like me because of my size. Then I thought, 'Well, I'm short and I wear glasses, too, but it hasn't occurred to me that they wouldn't like me because of that!'"

Pat smiled, "A person may not warm up to me for all sorts of reasons—they're shy and reserved, they're having a bad day, or they just prefer a different sort of person. The important point for me to remember is that their response expresses who they are and how they feel, not who I am or how I should feel. That's so liberating for me!"

It's important to remember that people's actions are largely dependent on what's going on inside them. None of us can see inside another person and know for sure what they're thinking or feeling. The old saying goes, "When we compare our insides to another person's outside, we are bound to lose." We especially can't know *why* they do what they do. A lot of people don't know enough about themselves to know what's going on inside even if they would tell us! One thing we can do is assume good faith and interact positively with those we meet. This may mean making one small degree of change in our attitude.

Marlene, at thirty-three, learned from her therapist that a lot can change as a result of one small alteration. Marlene realized that she had become too self-absorbed in how she imagined others may think of her bountifulness. She said, "I decided to smile at one person every day. It's not that I went around frowning, but since I assumed that I'd be rejected, I rarely made eye contact. I read an article that said a telephone salesperson who smiles while talking on the phone makes sales. I figured if I did the same—used smiles to create and communicate positive energy—I'd probably have better experiences with the people I met." It seemed ridiculously simpleminded, yet she was tired of her own grumpy attitude about life. Some people smiled back. Others didn't. But every single day, she felt just a little better about herself, and that impacted other parts of her life.

Assuming good faith can even turn a disagreeable situation into a pleasant one. Just ask sixty-eight-year-old Amy, who ran a stop sign and was pulled over by a police officer. As he approached the car, Amy remembered the last (and first) time she had been pulled over—some forty years earlier and many pounds lighter. Amy recalled batting her eyes and receiving only a warning from the officer. Amy reasoned, "But that was then, and this was now.

"The officer stood stoically at my window, asking for my identification and did I know why he pulled me over. I said that I did, and then, with my best, fullest smile, I told him about having been stopped forty years ago and never being pulled over since. I told him I thought that I had learned my lesson then without a ticket and that the officer had been so kind to me and and and . . . I went on and on, later realizing that I probably had been batting my eyes again, just on instinct. He hesitated, smiled, and gave me a warning rather than a ticket!" Was it his generosity or her charm?

Why contribute to the negativity so rampant in our world today by assuming bad faith or drawing the darkest interpretation of others' remarks? I realize there are critical, even cruel people who intend to harm others. For these people, strong self-protection skills are needed. But the majority of people you'll meet on a daily basis are focused on their challenges, not yours. They're obsessing on themselves, not you. So don't snarl or snipe. Lead with a smile, a little charm, and a great deal of tenacious good will. I guarantee that you'll have a much better time and meet fewer people who you perceive as finding fault with your size.

More Secrets for Bountiful Living

Change your behavior by one tiny degree. If you are on the road and change your trajectory by one degree, in one hundred miles, you will be almost two long miles from where the original path would have taken you.

→

Smile and make eye contact with one new person each day, for example, as Marlene did.

→

Assume the best intentions.

→

If someone says something to you that doesn't feel good, don't assume they are trying to hurt you. Simply repeat what they said. Many times people are unaware of the impact their comments may have. If they hear it back, they may do something differently.

→

Engage in "intentional dialogue," as presented
by Harville Hendrix, Ph.D., author of Getting
the Love You Want *and other books. Have the*
intention of hearing the other person until
you can understand their point of view
with compassion. You need not necessarily agree.
Mirror, validate, and empathize with what
you hear. You will make a connection
with the other person.

→

Sticks and Stones

I saw a man I had dated years ago. He looked
me over. I could tell he was taking in how large I
was. He said negatively, "Boy, you've sure
changed." I just laughed at him and said,
"Haven't we all! You used to be
*a real nice guy." —*TANZY

Some bountiful women rarely, if ever, hear negative comments. Perhaps there is something in the way they present themselves with a don't-tangle-with-me energy permeating the air around them. It's as if they have constructed an impenetrable space around themselves that protects them and keeps them feeling good about themselves. This active way of taking good care of yourself creates a positive way of moving about the world. The goal is not to act better than others, rather to simply state that we matter, we are entitled, we expect to be treated reasonably.

Yet all the positive thinking in the world doesn't completely eliminate the fact that some people say heartless, thoughtless, and sometimes staggeringly cruel things to larger people. Criticism from people we know can hurt the most, even when these comments are not specifically directed at us. A friend or colleague may comment about someone else who is big, not meaning to hurt our feelings, but revealing their true attitude about people of size in the process.

Judy, almost forty-six, had finished her Ph.D. in clinical psychology and was working under the supervision of another therapist named Jonah. She trusted him with her own story, as well as those of her clients, and assumed that he was accepting of her. However, one day Jonah was telling her a story and made the comment, "This enormous man came into the restaurant looking as if he could eat the entire smorgasbord." On he went with his story, unaware of what he had said or how it might impact Judy. Her immediate instinct was to confront him, "you know, educate him. But then I decided to wait and consider the consequences of taking on my supervisor. If the opportunity presents itself," she added, "I may discuss this with him. But until then, I'm biding my time."

Biding your time may mean biting your tongue, as thirty-eight-year-old Amy discovered while visiting a man recovering from liver cancer surgery in the hospital. As a minister, she and the other pastors at her church often made hospital visits. She told me, "I didn't really want to visit this man. My senior pastor had had a run-in with him, and asked me as a personal favor to go in his stead. I'd not met the man before, but I thought if he could offend the senior pastor, who is a pretty low-key kind of guy, there's no telling what I would encounter.

"It was even worse than I could ever have imagined! I had barely walked into the room when he started berating me for 'being so fat!' At first, I was stunned and speechless. I regained my composure and asked whether I could offer him some comfort or read to him from the *Bible*. He ignored those offerings and kept commenting on my weight, asking me how I could let myself go, on and on. I told myself that he was sick, unhappy, and probably frightened, and tried not to let him get to me.

"I prayed that he would stop, but he didn't. So I said gently, lovingly, and with tears welling up, 'I want to offer you support and encouragement. Please stop commenting about my weight. I am here to help you.' He stared at me." While she had succeeded in putting an end to his verbal abuse, she was nevertheless wounded by his remarks. When she left his room, she went to the hospital chapel and cried private tears. Once she had had a good cry, Amy went back to her church and tended to her next mission.

Amy's approach to receiving stinging, hurtful criticism was to respond lovingly, yet firmly. Other women have found that responding with a humorous, if not sarcastic, response gets their point across and leaves them feeling empowered. Tanzy told me about a painful comment she received while attending her college reunion. "I saw a man I had dated years ago. He looked me over. I could tell he was taking in how large I was. He said negatively, 'Boy, you've sure changed.' I just laughed at him and said, 'Haven't we all! You used to be a real nice guy.'" Score one for bountiful women.

Terry, an artist who loves going to the grocery store, in part because of the many colors, shapes, and patterns of the displays, had filled her basket with all sorts of delicious hors d'oeuvres, frozen items, and plenty of fresh ingredients to tempt the most discriminating palate. She said, "I had selected pâté, six or seven kinds of cheese, a large assortment of breads and crackers, herring, smoked salmon, chocolates—five or so varieties. There were gourmet chips, pretzels, chocolate-covered macadamia nuts, and cashews in my basket. As I rounded an aisle to purchase some wines, I heard one woman say to her friend, 'Did you see what that fat lady was buying? I bet she goes home and eats all of that herself.' I turned around, walked straight up to her, and said, 'I might.' Then I turned around and went back to shopping. I could have chosen to explain that I was having a party that night, but doing what I did was much more fun."

Recalling a similar moment from her life, Ramona said that when she was about eighteen, she had taken two young cousins with her to the movies. She said, "We were walking to the show when two young men went past. One of them yelled, 'There's the person who tackled me in the last football game.' I don't know where it came from, but out of my mouth came flying, 'No, it wasn't me, but I sure wish it had been!'" What a great line, a strong comeback while not decimating his character. She felt quite clever!

While a good one-liner can put an end to harassment, some bountiful women opt for a more demonstrative response. At thirty-three and concerned about her health, Florence goes for walks most days. Occasionally, someone will drive by and make a nasty comment. One time a car full of teenage boys was cruising along next to her as she went for her walk. They were calling out pig names and making ugly sounds. She said, "I pushed out my stomach and lifted my arms and made some horrific sound. They didn't know what to make of me, so they drove away. It tickled me for some reason, and as they sped off, I laughed and laughed."

When faced with these kinds of situations, it's important that we don't concern ourselves with the other person's feelings or try to help them "see the light." Our first priority is our feelings about ourselves and the way we live our lives. Sarah told me how she had coped with a cruel remark from a man walking by her on the street. "As he passed me, he said, 'Blubber, blubber, makes me want to shudder.' At first I couldn't feel a thing, I suppose because I could hardly believe he had said it! As it sunk in, I thought about the comment, over and over. I thought, 'You know, it's really quite poetic.' That made me smile. To diffuse its impact, I said it over and over and over until it simply lost its power."

While we're in the process of trying to change society's attitudes about bountiful women, we must acknowledge that making fun of large people is still part of our society. "Fat jokes may still be socially acceptable," declared Andy, a fifty-four-year-old secretary, "but I have the right to resent them. I used to cringe when I heard late night comedians, stand-up comics, and others make fat jokes. I find them demoralizing, demeaning, and, on some level, I feel personally annihilated.

"One night I was enjoying late night television and a comedian came on saying the most nasty and outrageous things. That was it for me. I was through being resentful. I decided to be radical and speak my mind. In fact, I'm on a personal crusade. I write a letter to every comedian, to every talk show host, to every newspaper with whom I encounter an offensive weight joke. I'm polite—no sense in being hostile. I simply tell them how much this kind of humor hurts." On some occasions, she has received a response. Some people have said they didn't realize how hurtful they were being. Mostly though, she hears nothing, but it makes her feel less lonely, less attacked, and less assaulted. It's a way for her to deal with these comments that are somehow acceptable to people with no personal experience in being large.

Perhaps one of the best ways to deal with unwelcome comments is simply not to acknowledge them at all. Rose, now seventy-two, has owned her own cake and pastry business for many years. She was talented and had a loyal clientele, doing business with some of the most elite people in her area. She was able to charge high fees for her work and make choices about the people she was willing to serve. Sometimes, though, she encountered a rather snooty person who would make disparaging comments to her.

She said, "I not only ignored the comments, I simply refused to hear them. My staff would sometimes speak up in my defense, but I went my way as if nothing had been said.

My size is fine with me. Anything to the contrary, I just do not hear, so it never wounds or affects me."

Not all people who are critical of larger people are thin. Even those of us who are bountiful can fling negative barbs at other large people or retain biases against those we perceive as "larger" than we. It takes a strong person to own up to such attitudes, but I found such a woman when talking to Ruth, a fifty-five-year-old entrepreneur. She grimaced and acknowledged, "I get upset when I think people discriminate against me, yet recently I found myself in that exact same role. I was developing my website and needed consultation. When I asked around for a referral, Sarah's name kept coming up. I called and arranged a meeting.

"I was surprised when she showed up at my office. Now I'm large. But Sarah was . . . larger! She showed me her work and it was brilliant. It was clear that she would do a superior job, but I hesitated to hire her. Sarah realized that I was put off by her size and brought up the topic. I was cornered but also glad and rather relieved that she'd said something. Before I could put my foot in my mouth and say something I may have thought but would have regretted voicing, I offered her the job."

Most comments that people make, or attitudes they hold, have nothing whatsoever to do with us as persons. Lee was released from feeling criticized when, "My therapist told me that, in this society, weight is one of the top three or four things about which people talk. That's just the way it is. I stopped taking the many comments others made about weight as a personal affront. I realized that their comments were simply not about me; they reflected what other people worried about. I no longer had to join them. What a freeing thought! I could simply hear what they said and let it go. What an amazingly refreshing way to think about it!"

It takes wisdom to know when to stand up for yourself and when to walk away, when to shut your ears and when to speak up, when to confront and when to point and laugh. We grow in wisdom as we experiment with solutions, observing what works best in specific situations. Give yourself permission to try out different ways of reacting to comments intended to wound you, refusing to be held captive by the attitudes or behaviors of others. Break free from any limitations you've set on yourself as well. You might be surprised by just how good if feels to zing a one-liner, act crazy and throw your harasser off balance, or simply point your nose in the air and walk elegantly by.

More Secrets for Bountiful Living

If someone says something hurtful, in a private moment tell them your feelings and what would work for you rather than storing or stuffing the feelings until you withdraw or attack.

→

Offer people who matter to you a compassionate way to relate to their fears or concerns about your size. For example, tell them to say, "I love you and want you to be okay." Sometimes people do not know how to speak to you.

→

Say to yourself, "I need to be grateful for the body I have. Disdain causes illness."
Or, as Deborah Burgard, Ph.D., says,
"Your body hears everything you are thinking. Think well of it."

→

Ignoring or avoiding hurtful situations may be best in certain situations.

→

Sometimes a private cry is what is needed.
Give yourself the chance to feel those feelings,
and then let them go.

➔

When the subject of weight (dieting, food) comes
up, do not take the subject personally as it is one
of the most frequently discussed topics.

➔

Enjoy a good one-liner retort. It's fine
to be a little "naughty."

➔

Section Four

Romancing and Dancing

Bountiful and Sexy

*I expect to be accepted. When I meet men, my
first thought is whether or not I'm interested in
them, not the other way around. It doesn't occur
to me to be insecure about my sexual
attractiveness. —ELVA*

Sure, many women are self-conscious about their bodies at
every weight, every age, every point in the monthly cycle. But
is it okay to feel, act, and be sexy, sensual, playful, mischie-
vous, and rebellious if you are bountiful? Do you have to
behave in a conservative, average, middle-of-the-road kind
of way if your body happens to be larger?

Not a problem for Tanya, who, at fifty, feels sexy and sassy
and ready to play. Tanya told me about a time when she ran
off for a weekend trip to Cape Cod with her friends Elaine and
Donna. This girls' weekend was made for relaxing, telling stories, and comparing notes about relationships, work, and life.
On the way out of Boston, they stopped to get some coffee
before the drive to the Cape. One very important thing to
know about Tanya is that she loves to flirt. She wears sexy
undergarments, thinks sexy thoughts, and is very aware of

her sensual and sexual self. She confided to me, "We trouped into the coffee place, and I spotted this attractive, polished man dressed in his three-piece suit. I started having sexy and playful thoughts about him in my head. I just smiled to myself and enjoyed the feeling. But before I knew it, I was doing a dramatic reading of the coffee and pastries menu.

"Elaine looked over at him and saw that he was mesmerized. It looked as if it was an exciting experience for him; he was caught up in the playfulness and sensuality of what was happening. She wanted to get us out of there because he might want to come along on our weekend adventure." All three ladies enjoy remembering the experience, not because of how the man responded, but because they all felt the exuberance and pizzazz of the moment. They have laughed and laughed in one of those you-had-to-be-there experiences as they recounted how luscious the pastries sounded and how much fun everyone seemed to be having.

Feeling sexy and good about yourself is certainly a bountiful way to live your life. Just because a woman is bountiful doesn't mean that she assumes she isn't desirable. For example, twenty-six-year-old Elva, a human relations person for a large corporation, told me "I expect to be accepted. When I meet men, my first thought is whether or not I'm interested in them, not the other way around. It doesn't occur to me to be insecure about my sexual attractiveness." Elva is the kind of bountiful woman who plays, invites, signals, and has a full dating life. No one would ever say she is anything less than beautiful and sexy.

Or consider Karen, a forty-four-year-old administrator in the police department, who, by her own description, carries more weight than her ideal. Karen loves the feel of silky clothes on her body; she loves to be touched and to touch. She is full of life and, given the opportunity, will choose to have sex if she wants to be with the person. Karen shows her body by wearing clothes that let people know she is a woman. While some women of various sizes do not want to be "girly girls," others do. Karen is one of those who does and has a great time.

Does she feel foolish? On occasion. Is it worth the enjoyment and sensual experience—yes! She sheds her share of tears, experiences self-doubts and discomfort, has her times of wondering why she has the body she has. Like many women, she has both a critic and a champion within her. Karen has confronted her critic, who shouts and tells her why she can't, shouldn't, won't be able to have a good time with the other side of herself. The champion, however, says, go for it, do it, go out and play; you deserve it. As she develops more awareness, Karen knows that she needs both voices, both aspects of herself. The critic has helped to keep her safe. The champion can lead her into exciting and sometimes scary situations. Balancing between the tension of her two sides will serve her best in whatever the present circumstance may be. Within the bounds of good judgment, embrace abundant experiences.

I also encourage you to open yourself to romance in unexpected places. MaryAnn never imagined that marshmallow peeps would become her romantic magnet. At fifty-eight and a retired nursing home administrator, MaryAnn loves yellow peeps after they have aged, like good wine. Ten months was the ideal amount of staleness, she admitted, if she could wait that long to eat them. MaryAnn's lifelong ritual was to wait until the day after Easter, go on a peeps pursuit, buy as many as she could find, take them home, slit open the top of the cellophane, and wait until they were magnificently chewy.

She described being on a peeps hunt four years ago. "I went out early Easter Monday to the local drugstore. I found myself next to a man who was filling his cart with my treasured yellow peeps. There are pink peeps and white peeps, but I adored only the yellow peeps. And he was taking them all!"

After a moment of panic, she gathered her wits about her. MaryAnn wondered how assertive, how aggressive she would have to be. As she slowly approached, she tried to figure out what to do. She explained, "At that moment, this guy looked up at me. He was reaching for more boxes, and I said, 'I'm here for the yellow peeps.' We locked eyes for a moment, an endless moment when I contemplated grabbing the boxes out of his hands, or even running off with his half-full cart. He said nothing, so I continued, saying that I coveted peeps when they were aged and chewy. He said he did too. And then we smiled."

They started chatting and he introduced himself as Fred. MaryAnn confessed to him that she kept her peeps in their "nursery," a rolltop desk in her study. Fred laughed and admitted that his preferred place was his wine storage because the temperature stayed constant. Neither of them had ever met anyone who even understood their devotion to these squishy little marshmallows gone dry. MaryAnn recalled, "I felt like I'd found my soul mate! I admitted that I was going to another store not far away for more peeps and asked if he wanted to join me. With a grin, Fred said he had had the same idea. So we went together."

Now, four years later, MaryAnn and Fred still shop for peeps together. They married, having been brought together by a mutual love. Where do you suppose they went for their honeymoon? Of course, to the Just Born factory in Bethlehem, Pennsylvania, makers of their luscious peeps.

Being yourself rather than trying to fit into arbitrary molds draws people with similar interests into your life. Albeit hard for the nonbeliever to imagine, MaryAnn has a true passion for those little chewy things, and she revealed her particular interest to Fred. How delicious that she met her match over peeps, then found what else they had in common.

Forty-year-old Belinda, an administrator for a group home serving children with developmental disabilities, met Bob, thirty-one, when he bought the car she had recently inherited from her uncle. When Bob was test-driving the car, they got to talking. Everything seemed easy and relaxed. Belinda thought he was kind of cute, but she had his driver's license so she knew how old he was and assumed that their age difference was a formidable obstacle to romance. Plus Belinda was large, while Bob was tall and trim. She gave up before anything could begin.

Fortunately for Belinda, Bob wasn't so easily deterred.

During the test-drive, he noticed some bike route maps in her car. Belinda aspired to riding a bike but had not gotten around to it. He asked her if she wanted to meet him for a bike ride that weekend. Not wanting to confess that she had not been on a bicycle in several years, she said, "Sure."

She recounted the tale: "At the appointed moment, I met him with dismay on my face. I was busted, as the kids say— my bicycle had two flat tires! Bob, being a truly generous man, fixed both tires without blinking an eye. Now the moment of truth. Off we went, and to my amazement, I did well. The peddles were turning and the sparks were flying!"

Their day out riding turned into a lively interlude. When Bob learned her age, he was surprised but nevertheless quite interested in pursuing an intimate connection. She said, "I always thought I had to be with a certain kind of man and here was someone so different—so much younger—than I had imagined. I'm a real city girl, and I've always seen myself with a go-getter businessman. But Bob is an account-ant, kind and loving. I might have turned away from him for all sorts of reasons, but I'm so grateful I took the chance. Even though I thought it would end quickly, now, nine months later, we are still spending loving time together."

While you may have a certain idea of who would make the best and right partner for you, being open to new options, being responsive to those people you meet, can invite unexpected experiences. Irene, twenty-nine, a graduate student in psychol-ogy, hadn't dated very much in her younger years. And she never felt particularly interested in the men she met. She blamed herself for who she chose, what she looked like, being too picky, having impossible demands, and on and on.

When she met Elena, she was intrigued partly because she was Russian, a medical student, and a musician. They became fast friends, spending time studying together, laughing, and comparing notes about all of life's questions. One day Elena told Irene how beautiful she looked. Irene, in typical fashion, brushed off the compliment. In the conversation that followed, Elena told Irene that she had been noticing her in a different way. While the idea of being romantically involved with a woman had not been in Irene's consciousness, she did love Elena.

As soon as Elena began to talk about her feelings, Irene felt at home, at ease, more peaceful than she had ever been before. For her entire life, she said, she had wanted to feel as she did with Elena. In a quiet knowing way, Irene said, "Being close with Elena touched my soul, touched me in a way that finally made my life make sense. I never knew I could be this peaceful with another person. I feel so fortunate to be with her." And now together, they have the life each has wanted.

It is natural to want to link with another person, a loving experience you need not deny yourself. Opportunities to develop intimacy can be overlooked if we assume we're unlovable or if we narrow our idea of who we might be able to love. Open your eyes and your heart. You may be pleasantly surprised at who appears in your life.

More Secrets for Bountiful Living

If you are acting old and matronly, stop. Being
large does not make you old. Acting old, limiting
what you do, will make you feel old.

→

Say to yourself, "Let me think about that" before
saying yes or no to the possibilities. Always
acting from instinct keeps you stuck where you
have always been.

→

Pay attention to how you feel when you do what
you do. Being conscious of your choices gives you
the chance to create the life you want.

→

If you are lost in your own self-assessment and
protection or in your judgments about other
people, you may miss what and who is right in
front of you. Give yourself and others a chance
to see what and who is near you, now.

→

To Flirt or Not To Flirt

*Two days later, to my surprise, I saw the
same man and he smiled again. This time
I wondered, "Is this guy dangerous or
is he just flirting? And if he is flirting
with me, is it for real or is he making
fun of me?" . . . Brave person that I am,
I decided to find out.* —JOANNE

Bountiful women flirt when they want to, and refuse to
arbitrarily disqualify themselves from romance on the basis
of their size. Sherrill, a journalist, had never been married
and, at the age of forty-eight, wanted someone with whom
to frolic, travel, and love. She met many interesting men in
her work, but she assumed her size was an obstacle to them
and thus shied away from letting any possibility of a relationship grow.

While attending a business dinner, Sherrill met Rob at her
table; they immediately clicked. They seemed oblivious to
everyone else in the room as they talked away throughout
the meal about their work and their lives. Time flew! Sherrill
told me, "I really, really liked this guy and wanted to spend

more time with him. Dessert had been served, and I knew the speaker would begin in five or ten minutes and the moment might be lost. I gathered my strength and said, 'Rob, talking to you has been great. I would enjoy getting to know you better. We seem to have so much in common. I am an up-front person. I wonder if my size is a barrier for you. If so, could we talk about it directly and not let it be a silent factor in whether or not we spend any more time together?'"

Whew! It was a mouthful, but at least the issue was on the table. "Then Rob said, 'Yes, your size was something I noticed, but now that you've brought it up, I feel better. I don't know what I think.' I felt as if I had stopped breathing. Then, after what seemed like forever, he added, 'Could we go for a walk in the morning, have breakfast and talk?' You bet we could! Yippee!"

Sometimes giving voice to the unmentionable, the unspeakable, makes it easier to deal with in a direct manner. Requiring the other person to initiate a challenging subject, especially in romantic relationships, may deter any connection. Taking the lead in the conversation can dispel unnecessary tension. If we're comfortable with the discussion, other people are more likely to relax also. And even if we're not completely at ease, we've had much more time to think about our size than this new person in our life has.

Of course, you have to be ready for the answer if someone does have trouble with your body. Better to know that at the beginning, though, and get it over with. No, it won't feel good, but never starting the conversation will keep you stuck where you are. Don't let your fears determine what you do.

Sharon, a hospital administrator, learned this the hard way—and nearly cooked herself to death in a spa! A colorful, lively person, Sharon and her friend went on vacation to a Club Med to meet men. While they didn't say this out loud, they both knew their agenda. Sharon could talk to anyone; she and her pal thought the concentration of people would be a good way to meet potential partners.

The second night into their week, her friend went dancing and Sharon went to the hot tub. She described the scene. "The water felt so good, warm and soothing. The stars were glistening, and I felt gloriously relaxed, alone in the tub. I was there quite a while when a good-looking man arrived to soak too. He was incredibly attractive to me, about the right age, and naturally and easily we began to chat.

"I don't mean to brag," Sharon hesitated, "but I feel like I have a very pretty face. Somehow I believed that since my body was submerged, he wouldn't notice that I was bountiful. He seemed genuinely interested in me. However, the water was hot, and I knew that I needed to cool down. But I didn't want to get out of the tub and let him see my body. I wished that I'd placed my robe and towel nearer to the tub so I could have covered myself more quickly and made a fast exit. I stayed longer and longer, until I felt like a cooked goose. What had been a relaxing hot tub experience had become uncomfortable and unpleasant.

"I hoped that I could outlast him, but he seemed so happy talking to me, I realized that he'd never get out of the tub. Still I waited and waited until I was about to pass out. I held on to the thought, 'I am attractive and valuable, inside and out,' and then said to him, 'I love talking to you, but if I stay one more minute I'll be ready to be served up for dinner. I feel like a cooked goose!' He laughed and I got out of the tub." After a quick "good night," Sharon assumed the worst and left feeling like he was no longer interested in spending time with her once he saw her out of the water. The rest of the night Sharon was miserable, imagining how awkward it would be to bump into him again in the small resort.

The next morning, Sharon spotted him with another woman. "Ugh," Sharon told me. "I thought, 'He has already found someone else more attractive to him.' My heart sank and I felt my eyes fill with tears.

"Then he saw me. I wanted to hide under the table. I wanted to disappear. He and the woman walked over to me and he said, 'Diane, this is the beautiful woman I met in the hot tub last night. Sharon, this is my sister. I've been raving about you all morning. Can we join you for breakfast?'"

Sharon learned a valuable lesson—do not assume rejection. She could have unwittingly eliminated any positive outcome by becoming haughty or defensive. No one wants to be hurt, but assuming that hurt is inevitable will keep us from possible positive experiences. Since none of us can read minds, we may miss out on a lot if we assume rejection.

Sharon enjoyed the company of her new friends for the duration of the vacation. Although a permanent romantic relationship never developed, Sharon still smiles when she reflects on the conversations she had with Richard—who obviously thought she was a beautiful woman just the way she was.

Sharon is not alone in assuming that romance is outside her grasp. Bountiful, successful, and outgoing, Joanne, a thirty-nine-year-old advertising copywriter living in New York City, realized that she had been making this same erroneous assumption. Devoting her life to her job, spending most evenings and weekends meeting demanding project deadlines, she was proud of her work but uncomfortable with herself, particularly as her weight increased year by year.

She told me about an experience that changed her thinking. "I was walking to work from the subway one day, when an attractive man seemed to flirt with me. He looked me in the eyes and smiled and nodded as if to indicate something positive. Now, I rarely make eye contact with anyone on the streets, so I wondered if I had made the whole thing up. I thought, 'He wasn't flirting with me, was he? No way.'

"Two days later, to my surprise, I saw the same man and he smiled again. This time I wondered, 'Is this guy dangerous or is he just flirting? And if he is flirting with me, is it for real or is he making fun of me?' Since I did not feel attractive, it was hard to imagine that he found me attractive. Well, I haven't gotten where I have in my job by being shy," Joanne smiled as she continued. "Brave person that I am, I decided to find out.

"I decided that if I ever saw him again, I'd smile and say hello. Even if it turned out poorly, I promised myself to take the chance. I had to wait almost two weeks, two long, long weeks, before I saw him again. You know, this is a big city. But even if I didn't see him again, I would always have this plan for the next person. Just having thought this through made me feel better, more energized, more hopeful about my life.

"Then I saw him again. I had rehearsed my plan so many times that I acted without thinking or hesitating. I smiled and said, 'Hello!' He responded with a hello, and we walked to my building, which, it turned out, was next to his. He introduced himself as Stan and suggested meeting for coffee, which we did."

Joanne and Stan talked about everything from puppets to petunias, from Mahler to Monaco. Before long, it was clear that they liked each other very much. By the time their coffee had grown cold, Stan asked Joanne to dinner. Laughing, Joanne said, "I actually had the nerve to ask him if this was a date! He smiled and said, 'Oh yeah!'" The end of the story? They were married seven months later at the church next to the buildings where they worked.

Regardless of the outcome of flirting, giving yourself the encouragement to take a risk, even if it turns out to be a tumble, is a chance to be alive. Staying safe can only result in maintaining the status quo. If you maintain the status quo, you actually go backwards because time is passing and opportunities are being missed. Plan. Stretch. Flirt. You've got nothing to lose by sharing a smile.

More Secrets for Bountiful Living

Dance like nobody's watching, and love like it's never going to hurt.

→

Hold on to two different points of view at the same time. When there are two people, there are (usually) two valid points of view, even if they are completely opposite each other.

→

Do not assume rejection or you will limit your opportunities.

→

Be good and kind to yourself and others by investing in indirect reciprocity, the concept that doing good deeds increases the likelihood that someone else will treat you better. When you are generous or friendly to another person, your world expands, creating an affirmative vortex for you and the people around you.

→

Creating a Safe Place to Meet Interesting People

Finding a place where you can be yourself,
in all of your glory, has myriad benefits.
You get to do something you enjoy, and you
may meet some other like-minded people.

What if you rarely meet people with romantic potential? What can a bountiful woman do then?

Joan, single at the age of thirty-one, works as an administrative assistant. While her career is rewarding, it does not fulfill all her needs, and she wants to marry and have children. Even though she has not dated much along the way, she decided that it was time to get going. She told me, "My challenge was finding a locale I considered comfortable where I could meet men. I saw my friends going to clubs wearing their little short skirts and tight shirts, but that wouldn't work for me. Even though I love to dance, I didn't feel comfortable in the night club atmosphere.

"So I looked for another way to move forward and decided that I enjoyed taking walks. I did not know my physical capacity, so I was hesitant to go on organized walks where other single people went, fearing I'd hold them back."

But Joan didn't let that concern derail her. She was determined to find a way that would work for her. Joan got the schedule for Sierra Club hikes in her area, and saw that both the length and the difficulty of the hikes were listed. She set her target on doing a beginning hike—modest distance and moderately flat terrain. She said, "I knew I could always meet the group for dinner after the hike if I couldn't keep up, but I thought I would be able to get to know people better, both men and women, if I spent time with them during the activity."

To prepare for the hike, Joan walked in her neighborhood each morning, something she had always intended to do anyway. Rather than set a specific goal, Joan walked as far as she could each day. She did not want to travel so far that she'd become exhausted, hurt herself, or allow herself to become discouraged. She took it slow, and each day she jotted down how long and how far she walked. Her eyes sparkled as she said, "To my surprise, it was really quite easy! Sometimes I listened to the radio, sometimes to tapes. Mostly I just looked around." She smiled, "I got the idea to make the walks a treasure hunt, discovering something new to incorporate in my art projects. What began as a 'man hunt' expanded into a treasure hunt, adding more to my life than I had imagined."

In a short time, she was ready. Joan went on an easy hike as a trial, and it was a breeze. Her confidence increased, and she was on her way. The next two hikes were so great and so enriching that she came to enjoy the hikes for their own sake and not just as a means to meet men. She has made several new friends on the hikes and has met a couple of interesting men. By moving forward in her life right now, not waiting until some imagined better time, Joan has attracted an array of positive experiences, including healthy movement, unexpected treasures, new people with whom to interact, and a place to meet men as well.

Similarly, Lee, a psychologist, decided that after being divorced for fifteen years, she wanted to have a committed relationship. The men she met through work, social activities, and friends were not available for one reason or another. So Lee used her imagination and creativity to meet men in a variety of ways. She asked her friends to keep their eyes open for appropriate men. She went to different social events, some with singles, others with mixed groups, and made a point of meeting people. One of the small newspapers In her community listed the fund-raising events that various groups were having each week. She reviewed those lists and selected groups for which she had an affinity, then called to volunteer during the actual event. Sometimes they needed help and other times they did not. Sometimes she took along a friend who also might be supportive of the cause. She was out and about with a commitment to herself to see whether she could meet someone who would be a good match for her.

While this could sound intense, Lee was having a great time and enjoyed the experience of doing things she had never done before and contributing to her community. Then she met Gary, a Southerner from High Point, North Carolina, at one of the fund-raisers. She told me, "I was smitten. He was tall and hunky, yet had a gentle way about him. I enjoyed his intelligence almost as much as those endearing dimples when he smiled. I definitely wanted to get to know this man!" The more they chatted, the more she liked him. She asked him if he was interested in meeting for coffee the next day. He said he was.

Lee decided that she was going to bring up their difference in physical fitness. Gary had spoken about skiing as a favored activity. Because she liked him she wanted to deal with any thoughts that might interfere with them getting to know each other. She has found that bringing up uncomfortable subjects early on and talking about each person's issues makes getting to know someone much easier for her. "My fitness level," Lee explained, "is not a taboo subject. So I brought up the topic and told him, 'If it is any discomfort for you, please say so.'" While some of her women friends thought bringing up the subject was too straightforward, Lee's openness meant that she could be herself—someone who was honest while looking to make a real and personal connection with the men she met. Gary said that what mattered to him were her beautiful blue eyes and curly blond hair. They have now been married for nine years.

Rather than join an existing group of single adults, you might want to start your own. Even if you're not overly outgoing, nearly anyone can invite people of like interests over for a scrumptious meal. Lenore, who at sixty-four has two grown children, works as an author and lives on her own in a major urban area. She loves to eat, cook, and be around people who love food, too, so being lively, she often entertains by hosting dinner parties. When she wanted to date again, she decided that having people gather for a fabulous dinner was the best way to meet people of similar interests.

Lenore started a group for "foodies"—people who love food. She put an advertisement in the local newspaper for single people who wanted company eating at great restaurants, then started a group that meets once a month to do just that. She books two tables for each dinner, with no particular assignment of men or women. They meet for drinks before dinner and coffee afterward. In between, they eat dinner, switching tables once during the meal.

She told me, "The Foodies Group turned out great. I've made some new women friends, and have had the chance to sample some of the best restaurants in town. I had dated several men I met through the group before I met Gregg at one of the dinners." After several years of dating, Lenore and Gregg married. She smiled, "The reception had the most exquisite food you might imagine a couple of foodies could arrange!"

Finding a place where you can be yourself, in all of your glory, has myriad benefits. You get to do something you enjoy, and you may meet some other like-minded people. Cecelia, a thirty-three-year-old dentist, was so busy that she didn't have much time to invest in meeting men. At the end of each day, she was so tired she wasn't sure how to go about meeting people.

Cecelia lived south of San Francisco where there is a coffee bar on almost every block. She began stopping at a local café after work for a simple cup of regular black coffee. As she showed up day after day, first one person and then another said hello to her. After a month or so, she had met at least a dozen people. Cecelia had had many doubts about her appearance, but in this setting where she felt absolutely no pressure to be or do anything except drink her coffee, she was able to talk and listen.

Many of the people, the "regulars" who came by each afternoon, also showed up on Saturday mornings, often with their dogs in tow. Cecelia enjoyed getting to know her fellow coffee drinkers and their beloved canines. One Saturday she showed up with Calvin, her endearing black Labrador puppy, who was an instant hit. She felt like she belonged, comfortable with Calvin at her side. Cecilia soon had a large group of people with whom she could be herself.

When she met Dan, she had no thoughts of being self-conscious. She was simply and wonderfully herself. Dan invited Cecilia to breakfast, and they took their doggies to a nearby outdoor cafe. A romance has begun.

Another way to meet people with romantic potential is to

ask friends and colleagues to introduce you to single people they know. Fifty-nine-year-old Evelyn, a nursery school teacher, didn't have a lot of opportunities to meet eligible men in her line of work, but she wanted to have a date for her sixtieth New Year's Eve—her last year teaching and the end of the millennium. Evelyn told me, "I had to laugh at myself, recalling how many times as a young woman I had fretted about having a date for New Year's and now, forty years later, I was having the same thoughts." Evelyn had dated over the years and was married for a brief period, but had mostly spent her life with friends and her now thirty-year-old daughter. This year, though, she wanted a date.

She recalled, "I thought of everyone I knew, anyone I might ask to be my date, even as a friend. I asked my friends if they knew of anyone. I looked around at church and even considered going to a singles' event to meet someone, but that seemed extreme since all I wanted was a date for one night." Looking at the situation from all angles, she considered having a party so she would be with other people, and imagined going to the party some friends of hers were hosting. Evelyn said, "I really wanted to dress up, look forward to, and celebrate the millennium with someone."

What did she do? At church, she saw a man who she had noticed at the services before. She said, "I know the pastor and his wife well, and they knew me to be a reasonable person. I wondered whether they would have any negative thoughts about me if I asked them about this man. But I wanted this so badly, almost in a schoolgirl kind of way, so I approached the pastor and told him my dilemma—that not since I was a girl had I looked forward to New Year's Eve, dressing up, going out, and would he help me obtain information about this man?" The pastor was more than happy to help and contacted the man, named Phil, about a New Year's Eve date. Phi, a widower, was delighted. After they were formally introduced, Phil asked Evelyn to be his date New Year's Eve! Since then, they have become friends who plan special events together. Evelyn is an inspirational example of a woman who has a vision for herself and goes after what she wants. Refusing to waver from her intention or judge herself in a way that diminished her energy, Evelyn declared, "I want this experience. I am going to find a way to make it happen." Many people, maybe more than you think, want to see you happy and would be willing to help out by introducing you to single friends. Letting your needs and desires be known is the first step in enlisting their help. Like Evelyn, you could soon be dating someone new, with a little help from your friends.

Another way to find romance is to "get on the Net." Bountiful women, like other women, have found this to be a good resource for meeting other people. On-line dating services are ever-growing resources for finding compatible partners. Ethel (named for her mother's look-alike, Ethel Mertz), a forty-four-year-old chocolate maker, had been an engineer and knew how to surf the web. On a late night search for chocolate sources, she digressed and went looking for an adventure. Kissed with a brilliant mind and a bountiful body, Ethel wrote a chocolate-based description of herself and posted it on several sites.

Not surprisingly, she received many replies, some of which she simply deleted. However, two of them caught her attention and she was on a roll. Ethel wrote a few brief notes to each of the men, then decided that she better meet them in person before she constructed fantasies around them. In her usual frank style, she told each of them that she was the size of actress Camryn Manheim, from the television show, *The Practice*. Both maintained interest and wanted to meet her. Ethel scheduled both dates on the same day, hoping that if one of them worked out, she would feel pleased. She couldn't imagine having to get herself psyched up to go out a second time if the first date didn't go well.

She chose the day after her birthday to meet them, because she figured that she would be feeling good the day after her party. The day arrived. Ethel admitted, "I spent more time than usual getting dressed so I would feel particularly spiffy. Off I went, feeling scared and excited too. When the first man, Roger, showed up, we had a nice time talking. My heart was pounding away as I watched, monitored, for any sign of rejection. Even under my watchful eye, I did not see anything but a cute, friendly guy."

After lunch, they went for a walk. He took out a small box, a birthday present, he said; it was a simple gold bracelet for her birthday. Ethel knew everything was going to be okay now—he had accepted her and she was smitten with him. As promised, she met the other man, but he was not of interest anymore. Being upfront, Ethel explained the situation, and he said to call him if it did not work out with Roger. It did, though. Roger and Ethel have recently launched a line of custom-made chocolates, created with a signature silver and gold dust. They are not only business partners, they are partners of the heart as well.

Being totally frank saves everyone time and pain. If your size is an issue, why bother? Move along. Go and meet someone else with whom it's not a concern. Remember, not all romances last forever, even for thin people! So if a relationship doesn't work out, it won't feel good, but the words, "my body didn't cut it," are less likely to creep into your thoughts. Dating can be bruising, but so is the alternative—not trying. And, as is true for the bountiful women who shared their stories with me, going for it can have lasting, loving rewards.

More Secrets for Bountiful Living

*Even if you feel scared or hesitant, reach out for
what you want to make your life better.*

→

*If you feel shy, get support in therapy,
a women's group, or from your friends.*

→

*Don't keep your desire to date a secret.
Tell people you know you want to meet someone.
Ask for help from those who are in contact
with a lot of people, such as a pastor, a rabbi,
or professor.*

→

*You will be in a crazy-making situation if you
say you want to meet someone and then do
everything to inhibit that from happening.
Go after what you actually want by tackling
the barriers.*

→

Friends or Lovers?

Not every relationship is destined for romance.
Sometimes the people we meet become friends
and companions along the journey.

Joelle, a realtor at thirty-six, was a go-getter kind of person. She could sell and she did—as long as what she was selling was real estate and not herself. Assuming that her size eliminated her from having a personal life, she concentrated on friendships, where she was known as "selfless to a fault." Then she met Mike.

Joelle sighed, "Mike was adorable, gregarious, successful, very easygoing. I was instantly attracted to him, but I was afraid that he would not be interested in me so I became his good friend. In fact, I think I hid from myself how attracted I was to him. I thought I was content with the buddy role.

"We'd get together and talk. I was helpful and supportive when he broke up with his girlfriend, you know, always there for him. He was there for me, too. We were buds. Once he was available, I didn't even talk to my friends about what to do because I was so concerned that he wouldn't be interested in me. And I couldn't see for myself how much he mattered to me. I had a dream one night that we were stranded on a desert island together. My psychologist sister had always been touting the importance of dreams as a way to know ourselves. I got the message.

"I knew I had to do something different. I wanted to know that he enjoyed my company, not just someone's company. So I took the initiative. I was so unsure about all of this, but I wrote him a note. When it came time to talk to him, I got the note out and read it out loud. 'Dear Mike, you are such a wonderful friend. I have a good time when we get together. I would like to see whether we can have a more personal relationship, maybe even a romance. I am nervous about saying this, which is why I had to write it down. I know that this has not been what our relationship has been about. Either way, I am glad to be friends, but this is what I would prefer.'"

Joelle was not completely sure she could continue her friendship if he turned her down, but she was ready to make a change. She knew that to be able to spend more time with him, she had to come forward and speak her truth in as clear a way as possible, or she would lose the friendship anyway. Mike's response was not what Joelle had been hoping for—he said that he didn't know what to say, that he didn't think of her in a romantic way. He asked for a couple of days to think about it.

Joelle saddened, "I felt dreadful as we went our separate ways. I wondered what I had been thinking, yet I also knew that I had to do this. He came by a few agonizing days later, and said that he didn't want to lose me as a friend, but he just didn't see me as a romantic partner. I withdrew from the friendship."

A week later, Mike called, but Joelle wasn't ready to see him again. She missed him, but felt too awkward and embarrassed about exposing her feelings and then feeling rejected. However, a month or so later, she sold a big house and wanted to celebrate with a friend. She called everyone she knew, but no one was free to go out spontaneously with her. Finally, with much ambivalence, Joelle called Mike.

Joelle confided, "It was so great to hear his voice, and he sounded so glad to hear from me, too. He said that he wouldn't miss the celebration and that dinner was his treat. The best thing about our relationship is that it survived the honesty, from both sides. In fact, when I married someone else two years later, I asked him to be my 'best person.' He's a great guy and a truly loving friend."

Not every relationship is destined for romance. Sometimes the people we meet become friends and companions along the journey. Such was the situation with fifty-seven-year-old Sally, who was alone after her husband died. Having been married for thirty-five years, she wondered whether she fit into the dating scene, but her friends encouraged her to get out and about.

She explained, "I knew I had to get out of the house, so I decided to go back to school even though I didn't know exactly what I wanted to study. I had a master's degree in education, but had only taught school for two years while in my twenties. I enrolled in two undergraduate courses at a local university, and walked into class surrounded by eighteen year olds, people young enough to be my children. They were friendly, but it was clear that I was the odd-woman out. On occasion, I'd see another older person on campus, but not in the classes I took. I assumed that they were faculty members rather than other students.

"In my second semester, I had a break in my schedule and decided to spend time in the student center. I enjoyed watching people coming and going. I saw a man I thought might have been about my age." Sally smiled, "And he was alluring too! He was not wearing a wedding ring. We circled each other for weeks.

"I was afraid to approach him, going through angst about my size, my age, my competence, my shyness. But in my mind I practiced going up to him and saying, 'Hello, I've been noticing you for a while now, may I join you?' When the time came, having practiced those words about a million times, they just spilled out of my mouth. He said, 'Sure!' and we chatted for a while." A bit discouraged that he didn't say anything else about getting together another time, she was determined to put herself out there again. The next time she saw him, having practiced with her friends, she said, "I enjoyed talking the other day, would you like to get some coffee with me?" He did, and they had a great time. Again he said nothing about another time.

Not being one to give up, she had one more effort left in her. She said to him, "I have enjoyed our chats. Since you have not mentioned another time, I wasn't sure if you were interested in our being friends. I am. What do you think?" Breathless, she smiled at herself for being so aggressive, definitely not her usual style. He said, "I would enjoy that, too. I have a partner, and I wasn't sure what you had in mind. I, too, have appreciated our talks and would like to see you more, now that you know I am in a relationship."

Having the ground rules clearly marked, Sally was able to make a new friend, someone with whom she could share her educational experience. For Sally, that was just what she needed at the time. But the friendship wouldn't have taken root if Sally had decided that she was unlikable because of her size, or if she had taken an indirect approach to the friendship.

Being indirect in order to lessen the chances of being hurt may feel safer, but it can also be lonelier. At fifty, Sandra, an accountant, was used to dealing with facts and figures. She wasn't comfortable with talking about feelings in any way, shape, or form. While she had many opportunities to be with men, she was always businesslike, and no one would have ever guessed that she wanted a relationship. She might invite a man over for a drink or dinner after working together, never letting him or herself have a clue that she was interested in any other kind of relationship.

Sandra confided, "Looking back now, I can see that, even if someone had been attracted to me, I was completely unaware and unavailable. I preferred to be alone, protected from any possibility of rejection." Playing it safe meant missing opportunities.

She continued, "Everything changed for me with David, a long-term client who had lost his wife five years earlier. I had helped him get his financial world together in significant ways. He was grateful to me and liked me, but I never saw his affection as more than friendship.

Jane, my secretary, said, 'He's such a kind, nice man, I'm surprised he has not found a new wife.' I thought to myself, 'Yes, and why not with me?' I was shocked at myself when I heard that idea in my head. The next time I saw him, I asked if he was thinking about a new relationship, which might have an impact on his financial planning. There must have been something in my voice that signaled to him that it was safe to be more vulnerable, more honest, more personal. I shifted inside to allow a bit more room for my personal self, not just my business self to show. I held his eyes just a second longer and turned my shoulders toward him. I did this consciously, feeling a bit manipulative, but also like I wanted him to see me differently. He said, 'I've been wondering if sometime we might have dinner together.' I, of course, said 'Yes.'"

Sometimes we think we must totally reveal ourselves in order for someone to notice us. That may be true in certain circumstances. Yet in some relationships, taking a little risk is all it takes for romance to take root. Make eye contact, hold someone's eyes an extra fraction of a second, turn your body one degree more in their direction, slow the pace of your speech by an imperceptible amount, lower the register of your voice—shift something. People get the message that a different feeling is coming from you, even if they cannot pinpoint what has changed. A genuinely solid friendship can survive the question, "Is there potential for more between us?" And you may find that the best romances begin as friendships.

More Secrets for Bountiful Living

Take a chance.

→

See if you are in a two-choice dilemma, where you actually want two competing outcomes. You may want someone to like everything about you, but you also want them to be honest about their feelings about you. Decide what you actually prefer and tell the other person—you might not get to have both.

→

Make a small signal that expresses your interest in another person. You can increase the energy you direct toward that person by making eye contact and holding your gaze for a fraction of a second longer than usual, by turning your shoulders or body slightly more in their direction, or by touching them softly on the arm.

→

*Practice the words you want to say to someone,
a million times if you need to, so you can
actually say them, as Sally did.*

→

*If you say the unmentionable, and talk about
your size, you make it easier for both of you to
deal with whatever issues exist.*

→

*Be compassionate with yourself. Be
compassionate with the other person, too.*

→

Love Comes in All Sizes

*Knowing what it's like to be completely accepted
is an experience that changes you forever.*

Is love available only to women who fit the petite, thin stereotype? Is it possible for a bountiful woman to be loved, truly loved?

I asked that question of Christine, now forty-one and in her second marriage, who at one point believed that she was unworthy of accepting love. She said, "My first husband never approved of my weight gain. In fact, I think that's one of the main reasons the marriage ended." Looking back on that painful time in her life, Christine explained, "We met when I was thin, when he thought I was beautiful, intelligent, and desirable. But as I gained weight over the years, he became more and more critical, even cruel. When he left me, I was devastated."

After the divorce, Christine lost weight, convinced that only thin women can find love. She met another man and they began dating. Once again she began to gain weight, and her new love told her outright that he wasn't sexually attracted to her anymore. She recalled, "This time I said to myself, 'I may be alone for the rest of my life, but it is better to walk away than to be with someone who makes me feel this bad, this terrible.'" And she did.

Soon after, Christine met Jim, whom she later married. Jim was the first man she met when she was bountiful. She smiled, "I told him from the start about my struggle with weight, and he was totally supportive of my living life my own way. He accepts me no matter what size I am. Jim is handsome, successful, friendly, and makes me feel so loved. He is the first man in my life that I've been fully naked in front of, physically and emotionally, without hesitation. This is a tremendous freedom. I never had that before, even when I was smaller, and I would never settle for anything less now that I know how it feels to be loved."

Knowing what it's like to be completely accepted is an experience that changes you forever. One woman I spoke with, Susan, who is eighty-years wise, has been around the world and on her own most of her life. However, for fifteen years, she enjoyed a love-filled marriage that ended when her husband died. Gazing back in time, Susan sighed, "He told me that he loved my full, round, luscious body. In fact, he'd embarrass me sometimes by pointing out to his friends how delicious and sexy I was. Those were his words—delicious and sexy. But I was willing to be embarrassed because I loved how he enjoyed me and my full body. When he died, it was a great loss to me, but I never forgot how it feels to be loved like that."

With or without a partner, Susan takes her large, lovable self into the world without hesitation or apology. She's what some people would call "a character"—she drinks whiskey, tells bawdy stories, and makes everyone laugh. When Susan and I first met, she was sixty-five and eating at the counter of a rather posh restaurant that I also frequented. Introducing herself, she told me she was there to meet men. She said she imagined that her backside looked pretty inviting as she sat on that barstool eating her elegant dinner. She must have been right since she always seemed to have a man nearby.

Susan said, "I love having a good time, and I'll say or do just about anything to make that happen!" I found that to be true. While sitting at the bar with her, she would gaze into men's eyes and say the most scandalous things. One evening when we were having our weekly dinner, a man, who must have been twenty years younger than she, sat down next to her. She said her usual hello and asked him what he was drinking. She bought him a drink, introduced him to me, and soon we were all talking animatedly about life in the big city. In what seemed like a minute, she had asked him whether he was on his own, versus having a wife or girlfriend, and asked whether he wanted to join us for after-dinner drinks and a walk. He joined us that night and many others. They soon had private dinners together and became lovers.

She jokes and makes fun of herself, her age, and whatever else crosses her mind. On being large, she simply says, "There is more to love."

Not all of us have Susan's romantic confidence. Coming to believe we're worthy of love can be a struggle for many bountiful women. Sarah, a thirty-four-year-old housekeeper, has been large all of her life. Recently, her five-year relationship petered out because neither she nor Bill had much energy for it. She thought they stayed together because neither felt they could find anyone better. Sarah began seeing a therapist and as her self-esteem increased, she knew she wanted and deserved a more satisfying relationship. So she left Bill and is dating again.

Sarah asserted, "I'm not ready for a long-term commitment right now, so I'm dating two men. I felt so unappreciated by Bill for so long that seeing myself as desirable was nearly impossible. But the two men in my life now are giving me the chance to experience something altogether different." One man, Avram, truly loves her, her body, her entire being. She feels they celebrate being together emotionally and sexually. He responds emphatically to her, enjoying every bit of her.

She is also dating Steve, with whom she feels less compatible because of their religious differences, but whose company she enjoys immensely. She explained, "I want to date both men before I get serious again with anyone. This will give me the chance to come to terms with past experiences and learn to accept myself more. I look at myself in the mirror differently. Even friends say I carry myself differently, with more confidence and sexual energy. When these men tell me that I'm beautiful and they're honored to be with me, I believe them!"

Some of the bountiful women I've spoken with express how difficult it can be to believe that a man genuinely loves them and finds them attractive. Even Florence, now thirty-three, an accomplished website developer, who has been married to her high school sweetheart for many, many years admitted, "It was a long road to my accepting that he truly found me sexy. I guess that is due, in part, to the fact that he finds other women of differing sizes attractive as well. Finally I thought, 'What good is it doing me to doubt him? Why not simply enjoy his love?'" Florence brings up a very good point—why not accept, enjoy, and believe in the love given to us? We deserve it as much as anyone else. Romance is the spice of life and a wonderful ingredient to living bountifully.

More Secrets for Bountiful Living

Choose carefully and wisely the people with
whom you share your time and love. You deserve
to be cherished.

→

Use your time in ways that are enriching to you,
and be with men and women who offer what you
actually want.

→

Try out relationships with people you never
would have imagined yourself with. They may
work for you in ways you hadn't considered. If
not, let them go and move on.

→

When you are, feel, or do something awesome,
believe it when people tell you so.

→

Say to yourself, "This life begins and ends
with me."

→

It Begins and Ends with You

*Making the conscious choice to be more
visible when our impulse to hide can
help us live bountifully.*

We have come full circle, beginning with ourselves and now coming back to the central issue—how well do we love ourselves? How can we expect others to accept us if we don't accept ourselves first? If we are to live bountifully, the impetus must emerge from within us, and our direction must be guided by a personal vision, a personal determination to have the life we want.

What do you want for your life? Shame, defensiveness, and self-condemnation? Of course not. We all want to live bountifully, fully, freely. And women all over the world, regardless of their size, are experiencing this way of living. We can choose to hide or get involved, shrink back and limit our lives in shame or strut our stuff.

A good example of someone who jumps in the deep end is forty-six-year-old Karen, an evaluator in the court system. She said, "I received an invitation to my high school reunion and, even though I had had a good time in high school and there were many people I wanted to see, my appearance had changed and I was nervous about attending. Plus I was divorced and didn't want to explain all that.

Nevertheless, I decided that I really wanted to go, so rather than going with my first impulse—running away—I decided to be more visible and more involved and took an active role in the reunion. This gave me a basis to meet with other alumni, and allowed me to feel less self-conscious. I joined the planning committee, had a range of duties to complete, and was happily involved with the entire experience rather than letting the reunion destroy my self-confidence. I had a fabulous evening!" Making the conscious choice to be more visible when our impulse is to hide can help us live bountifully. Karen discovered that by being fully involved with her former classmates, she was less obsessed with her own insecurities.

Ramona is another bountiful woman who finds freedom in being proactive. As I spoke with Ramona, I realized she gives "visible" an altogether new meaning. Ramona recalled, "I was in an encounter group some years ago when the issue of my weight came up, and the group members—including some artists—all started urging me to model in the nude for that handful of artists. At first I was appalled by the idea. I'm not very showy, and wasn't even when I was thin years before. The assistant therapist said something very profound and helpful. He said, 'That's the only body you have and you'd better like it.' That really struck me deeply.

"So I did it. I actually posed in the nude. I was so nervous sitting there that I was perspiring like mad, the sweat was dripping off of me. A couple of the people went out to the garden, got flowers, and put them in my hair and one in my belly button. That broke the tension, and I actually relaxed and started enjoying the experience. Plus the drawings were lovely. I had never seen myself the way they saw me. I was so surprised at how beautiful I looked."

I wondered how she found the courage to model in the nude. She said, "I had two choices, take advantage of this unique opportunity or just run away. I didn't want to run, so I chose to celebrate myself instead. It gives me goose bumps to talk about it." This experience may not be for everyone. Ramona, nevertheless, found deep meaning in it, both from the words and from seeing her body appreciated, accepted, and made magnificent from those artists' perspective. She felt deep awareness of their eyes on her, knowing that they saw her as worthy, splendid, and large.

Do you have rules inside your head that keep you from connecting your bountifulness with other states of being—such as being loved, being worthy, being beautiful, being in the moment? A lot of women have such notions, even a list of "rules" for bountiful women. Some are funny and absurd, others poignant and telling, all reflect the experiences these women have endured. When you examine them closely, most of them must be discarded or, at the very least, reevaluated. Maybe these will resonate with you:

- Bountiful women should not eat dessert—except fruit, without whipped cream.
- Bountiful women should not eat potato chips, especially not directly from the bag.
- Bountiful women should not expect the same treatment as thin people.
- Bountiful women should eat less.
- Bountiful women should "weight" to live their lives.

Seeking perfection is a problem for many bountiful women and perhaps all women. Olivia, a twenty-seven-year-old engineer with a Ph.D., was convinced that she had to do everything perfectly. She selected a highly exacting career that was dominated by men. With dedication and determination, Olivia was excellent at what she did, having always been an overachiever. In her family, getting superior grades was expected, and she had always met their expectations.

She sighed, "I've finally learned that I do not have to be outstanding at everything. While this concept is anathema to my parents and most of my academic friends and associates, I'm giving myself permission to be *ordinary* at some things. I'm discovering that I love music. Instead of working sixteen hours a day, I'm taking piano lessons. And I don't have to get every note right. My fingers are large, so sometimes I feel awkward, but I love the sounds. What joy making music brings me."

We do not have to be perfect, nor overachievers, nor thin. All we need to do is be ourselves and love our bodies. Debby, at forty-one, shared some thoughts she uses for accepting and appreciating her body and the bodies of other bountiful women. She said, "My body is the very platform for being alive while on this planet, the reason I am alive. I feel loyal to my body now, like I want to protect it from the hostility out there. It has been very good to me—sensual, athletic, expressive, resilient. It feels good to be in this skin."

We all have the choice to live our dreams or sit around wishing, welcome love or shrug it away. There is no *real* reason to let your size deter you from reaching your goals or limit your options—only arbitrary judgments that become true if you make them so. The world is big enough for all of us, but time passes quickly. Live your life—now and bountifully—for this is the only life and body you've got.

Acknowledgments

Naturally, my heartfelt appreciation goes out to each woman who so freely spoke to me about her experience. To me, a good person helps others, helps to make the world a little better. Every single person in this book offered their story with that intention. I hear the chorus of their voices in my head, cheering each other on, and I am awed and honored by their experiences, their imagination, and the poignancy of what they had to say. It is a privilege to know you all. Thank you.

There are people who have supported me in my own process, my personal growth. To those who have helped me become who I am today, I thank John Beletsis, Ph.D., Florence F. Bernell, Grace Brown, Grace Lee Brown, Marilyn Bryson, Sylvia Feinstein, Joanne Gaffney, Barbara Green, James Hagan, J.D., Ph.D., Harville Hendrix, Ph.D., Peter Klein, Ph.D., John Livingstone, M.D., Eleanor Lusignan, Peter Pearson, Ph.D., Donna M. Ritz, Hal Stone, Ph.D., and Sidra Stone, Ph.D. I am fortunate to have been touched by each of you.

To those who have supported and encouraged this project, I thank Deborah Burgard, Ph.D., with whom I spent hours and hours, days and days, with doggies at hand, conceptualizing and considering the ideas in this book; Dana Schuster and Lisa Tealer, owners of Women of Substance Health Spa, for participating, encouraging, and caring about me and women of substance; Roberta Rasmussen, Ph.D., who participated, laughed, sat with me, and took an amazing number of photographs.

I offer many thanks to the Wildcat Canyon Press team, including Leyza Yardley, who calmly and thoroughly took care of so many requests; Tamara Traeder, my publisher, who filled in the blanks and did a whole lot of a whole lot; and Roy M. Carlisle, my editor, who has encouraged me to write for at least ten years, has never wavered, has taught me in ways I could receive, directed me, coached me, and heard my every concern; I am deeply moved, thank you.

I also thank Carmen Renee Berry for so much encouragement, belief in the project and me—a total unknown to her—for her writing, patience, and love of the women who speak in these stories, my heart is filled by how she responded to their tales.

About the Author

For more than twenty years, Bonnie L. Bernell has been a licensed psychologist and is currently in private practice with offices in Palo Alto and San Jose, California. She sees women, men, and couples, individually and in groups, and offers workshops on: Bountiful Women; Fun/Play/Joy for Women!; and Getting the Love You Want [based on the book by Harville Hendrix, Ph.D.]; Hot Monogamy [based on the book by Pat Love, Ed.D.]; and Voice Dialogue [based on the books by Hal Stone, Ph.D., and Sidra Stone, Ph.D.].

She has a doctorate and a master's degree in counseling from Lehigh University, Bethlehem, Pennsylvania, a bachelor's degree in psychology from the University of Wisconsin, Madison, and is an adjunct professor of counseling psychology in the graduate programs at Santa Clara University and the Institute of Transpersonal Psychology. She is a member of the American Psychological Association, California Psychological Association, and Santa Clara County Psychological Association. While she has written for her professional community, this is her first book for bountiful women. She is an artist working in paper. She currently lives in Palo Alto, California, with her husband and their border terrier, Grace Lee Brown.

View Bonnie's websites at: www.BonnieBernell.com or www.BountifulWomen.com.

About the Press

Wildcat Canyon Press publishes books that embrace such subjects as friendship, spirituality, women's issues, and home and family, all with a focus on self-help and personal growth. Great care is taken to create books that inspire reflection and improve the quality of our lives. Our books invite sharing and are frequently given as gifts.

For a catalog of our publications, please write:

Wildcat Canyon Press

2716 Ninth Street

Berkeley, California 94710

Phone: (510) 848-3600

Fax: (510) 848-1326

Email: info@wildcatcanyon.com

Visit our website at www.wildcatcanyon.com

More Wildcat Canyon Press Titles

LIFE AFTER BABY: FROM PROFESSIONAL WOMAN TO BEGINNER PARENT
An emotional compass for career women navigating the unfamiliar
seas of parenthood.
Wynn McClenahan Burkett
$14.95 ISBN 1-885171-44-7

STEPMOTHERS & STEPDAUGHTERS: RELATIONSHIPS OF CHANCE, FRIENDSHIPS FOR
A LIFETIME
True stories and commentary that look at the relationship between
stepmother and stepdaughter as strong, loving, and a life-long
union.
Karen L. Annarino
$14.95 ISBN 1-885171-46-3

AND WHAT DO YOU DO? WHEN WOMEN CHOOSE TO STAY HOME
At last, a book for the 7.72 million women who don't work outside
the home—by choice!
Loretta Kaufman and Mary Quigley
$14.95 ISBN 1-885171-40-4

40 OVER 40: 40 THINGS EVERY WOMAN OVER 40 NEEDS TO KNOW ABOUT
GETTING DRESSED
An image consultant shows women over forty how to love what they
wear and wear what they love.
Brenda Kinsel
$16.95 ISBN 1-885171-42-0

GUESS WHO'S COMING TO DINNER: CELEBRATING CROSS-CULTURAL, INTER-
FAITH, AND INTERRACIAL RELATIONSHIPS
True-life tales of the deep bonds that diversity makes.
Brenda Lane Richardson
$13.95 ISBN 1-885171-41-2

OUT OF THE BLUE: ONE WOMAN'S STORY OF STROKE, LOVE, AND SURVIVAL
A must read for stroke survivors and their families.
Bonnie Sherr Klein
$14.95 ISBN 1-885171-45-5

STILL FRIENDS: LIVING HAPPILY EVER AFTER...EVEN IF YOUR MARRIAGE FALLS
APART
True stories of couples who have managed to keep their friendships
intact after splitting up.
Barbara Quick
$12.95 ISBN 1-885171-36-6

CALLING TEXAS HOME: A LIVELY LOOK AT WHAT IT MEANS TO BE A TEXAN
Bursting with fascinating trivia, first-person accounts of frontier
days, curiosities, and legends of the people of Texas.
Wells Teague
$14.95 ISBN 1-885171-38-4

CALLING CALIFORNIA HOME: A LIVELY LOOK AT WHAT IT MEANS TO BE A
CALIFORNIAN
A cornucopia of facts and trivia about Californians and the
California Spirit.
Heather Waite
$14.95 ISBN 1-885171-37-4

CALLING THE MIDWEST HOME: A LIVELY LOOK AT THE ORIGINS, ATTITUDES,
QUIRKS, AND CURIOSITIES OF AMERICA'S HEARTLANDERS
A loving look at the people who call the Midwest home—whether
they live there or not.
Carolyn Lieberg
$14.95 ISBN 1-885171-12-9

BREASTS: OUR MOST PUBLIC PRIVATE PARTS
One hundred and one women reveal the naked truth about breasts.
Meema Spadola
$13.95 ISBN 1-885171-27-7

I WAS MY MOTHER'S BRIDESMAID: YOUNG ADULTS TALK ABOUT THRIVING IN A BLENDED FAMILY
The truth about growing up in a "combined family."
Erica Carlisle and Vanessa Carlisle
$13.95 ISBN 1-885171-34-X

THE COURAGE TO BE A STEPMOM: FINDING YOUR PLACE WITHOUT LOSING YOURSELF
Hands-on advice and emotional support for stepmothers.
Sue Patton Thoele
$14.95 ISBN 1-885171-28-5

CELEBRATING FAMILY: OUR LIFELONG BONDS WITH PARENTS AND SIBLINGS
True stories about how baby boomers have recognized the flaws of their families and come to love them as they are.
Lisa Braver Moss
$13.95 ISBN 1-885171-30-7

AUNTIES: OUR OLDER, COOLER, WISER FRIENDS
An affectionate tribute to the unique and wonderful women we call "Auntie."
Tamara Traeder and Julienne Bennett
$12.95 ISBN 1-885171-22-6

THE AUNTIES KEEPSAKE BOOK: THE STORY OF OUR FRIENDSHIP
A beautiful way to tell the wonderful story of you and your auntie or niece.
Tamara Traeder and Julienne Bennett
$19.95 ISBN 1-885171-29-3

LITTLE SISTERS: THE LAST BUT NOT THE LEAST
A feisty look at the trials and tribulations, joys and advantages of being a little sister.
Carolyn Lieberg
$13.95 ISBN 1-885171-24-2

girlfriends: INVISIBLE BONDS, ENDURING TIES
Filled with true stories of ordinary women and extraordinary friendships, girlfriends has become a gift of love among women everywhere.
Carmen Renee Berry and Tamara Traeder
$12.95 ISBN 1-885171-08-0
Also Available: Hardcover gift edition, $20.00 ISBN 1-885171-20-X

girlfriends FOR LIFE: FRIENDSHIPS WORTH KEEPING FOREVER
This follow-up to the best-selling girlfriends is an all-new collection of stories and anecdotes about the amazing bonds of women's friendships.
Carmen Renee Berry and Tamara Traeder
$13.95 ISBN 1-885171-32-3

A girlfriends GIFT: REFLECTIONS ON THE EXTRAORDINARY BONDS OF FRIENDSHIP
A lively collection of hundreds of quotations from the girlfriends books series.
Carmen Renee Berry and Tamara Traeder
$15.95 ISBN 1-885171-43-9

A COUPLE OF FRIENDS: THE REMARKABLE FRIENDSHIP BETWEEN STRAIGHT WOMEN AND GAY MEN
What makes the friendships between straight women and gay men so wonderful? Find out in this honest and fascinating book.
Robert H. Hopcke and Laura Rafaty
$14.95 ISBN 1-885171-33-1

INDEPENDENT WOMEN: CREATING OUR LIVES, LIVING OUR VISIONS
How women value independence and relationship and are redefining their lives to accommodate both.
Debra Sands Miller
$16.95 ISBN 1-885171-25-0

THOSE WHO CAN...COACH! CELEBRATING COACHES WHO MAKE A DIFFERENCE
Inspirational stories from men and women who remember a coach who made a lasting difference in their lives.
Lorraine Glennon and Roy Leavitt
$12.95 ISBN 1-885171-49-8

THOSE WHO CAN...TEACH! CELEBRATING TEACHERS WHO MAKE A DIFFERENCE
A tribute to our nation's teachers.
Lorraine Glennon and Mary Mohler
$12.95 ISBN 1-885171-35-8

THE WORRYWART'S COMPANION: TWENTY-ONE WAYS TO SOOTHE YOURSELF AND WORRY SMART
The perfect gift for anyone who lies awake at night worrying.
Dr. Beverly Potter
$11.95 ISBN 1-885171-15-3

DIAMONDS OF THE NIGHT: THE SEARCH FOR SPIRIT IN YOUR DREAMS
Combines the story of "Annie" with a therapist's wisdom about the power of dreams.
James Hagan, Ph.D.
$16.95 ISBN 1-879290-12-X

Books are available at fine retailers nationwide.

Prices subject to change without notice.